TWAYNE'S WORLD AUTHORS SERIES

A Survey of the World's Literature

Sylvia E. Bowman, Indiana University

GENERAL EDITOR

NIGERIA

Joseph Jones, University of Texas

EDITOR

Wole Soyinka

(TWAS 256)

TWAYNE'S WORLD AUTHORS SERIES (TWAS)

The purpose of TWAS is to survey the major writers —novelists, dramatists, historians, poets, philosophers, and critics—of the nations of the world. Among the national literatures covered are those of Australia, Canada, China, Eastern Europe, France, Germany, Greece, India, Italy, Japan, Latin America, the Netherlands, New Zealand, Poland, Russia, Scandinavia, Spain, and the African nations, as well as Hebrew, Yiddish, and Latin Classical literatures. This survey is complemented by Twayne's United States Authors Series and English Authors Series.

The intent of each volume in these series is to present a critical-analytical study of the works of the writer; to include biographical and historical material that may be necessary for understanding, appreciation, and critical appraisal of the writer; and to present all material in clear, concise English—but not to vitiate the scholarly content of the work by doing so.

Wole Soyinka

By ELDRED DUROSIMI JONES

University of Sierra Leone

Twayne Publishers :: New York

FOR W. S.

OUR W. S.

Preface

A biography or a definitive edition of Soyinka's work at this time would be as premature as the accounts of Mark Twain's funeral. He is at the height of his productive powers and will no doubt add considerably to the existing corpus of his work. This book pretends to be neither complete nor definitive. Rather it is a tentative offering of one man's reading of a writer whose work has intrigued and fascinated him. It cannot be final even for me since successive readings of the author's work continue to produce new insights. Phrases like "for me" in my interpretations convey the only sort of authority claimed for my readings.

I have of course benefited in my reading from such criticism as there is of Soyinka's work, and I have acknowledged direct indebtedness to particular critics. I have discussed Soyinka in conferences and seminars with colleagues and students in Africa, Europe, the United States, and Canada, and many of these discussions have given me fresh insights and points of departure for which I am grateful.

Some people have given me help of a personal nature which I gratefully acknowledge. Wole Soyinka himself has always kindly sent me unpublished material when I have asked him, but I have deliberately refrained from questioning him about his intentions in any work of art, preferring to take the works as offered even at the risk of misreading them. This is a risk every reader has to take and a danger every writer runs. Mrs. Valerie Land, while she was in Lagos, and Mr. Martin Banham both helped me with local material in Nigeria. Mrs. Anne-Marie Heywood very generously showed me some unpublished notes on the author which I found most illuminating. Professor Bernth Lindfors sent me copies of some published but little known short stories of Soyinka as well as copies of the two radio plays. For all this help I am enormously grateful.

For the actual writing of the book I am specially indebted to the Council of Canadian Universities for a totally unlooked-for and generous fellowship which enabled me to take time off from teaching while I wrote it. My own College Council of Fourah Bay with the enthusiastic support of my Principal Canon Harry Sawyerr gave me leave of absence on generous conditions. Without the help of these two bodies this book would still have been in the form of notes. My thanks to them are deep and sincere. As usual, my wife typed the manuscript of this book. For her loving care and valuable suggestions I am eternally grateful.

For the section on "Poems From Prison" I have used material which appeared in my review of these poems in *African Literature Today*.

ELDRED D. JONES

New College, Toronto &
Fourah Bay College, Freetown

Contents

Chronology

(Note: Only first or specially notable productions of plays are given.)

1934   Born in Abeokuta of Ijegba parentage.

1938-1943   Primary education at St. Peter's School, Ake, Abeokuta.

1944-1945   Abeokuta Grammar School.

1946-1950   Government College, Ibadan.

1952-1954   Student at University College, Ibadan (now the University of Ibadan).

1954-1957   Student at the University of Leeds, obtained B.A. (Honors in English). Short stories published: "Madame Etienne's Establishment," "A Tale of Two Cities." Another story also called "A Tale of Two Cities."

1957-1959   Attached to the Royal Court Theatre, London, as play reader. "The Invention" (never published) performed at the theater on November 1, 1959. On the program were also excerpts from *The House of Banigeji* and *A Dance of the African Forests*.

1959   *The Swamp Dwellers* produced in London; *The Swamp Dwellers* and *The Lion and the Jewel* produced in Ibadan, Nigeria.

1960   Lagos. Formed "The 1960 Masks," drama company. *A Dance of the Forests* produced in Lagos. The play won *Encounter* independence play award. Langston Hughes's *African Treasury* published containing Soyinka poems.

1961-1962   Rockefeller Research Fellow, Ibadan University.

1962   Francess Ademola's *Reflections* published containing pieces by Soyinka.

1962-1964   Lecturer at University of Ife.

1963   Satirical revue, *The Republican,* performed by "The 1960 Masks." Later in the same year *The New Republican* performed. *The Lion and the Jewel* and *A Dance of the Forests* published. Gerald Moore and Ulli Beier's *Modern Poetry from Africa* (Penguin) published containing Soyinka poems.

1964   Orisun Theatre (drama group) formed. *The Strong Breed,* a twenty-five-minute adaptation filmed in Nigeria for American television (Esso World Theatre). *The Strong Breed* and *The Trials of Brother Jero* produced at Greenwich Mews Theatre in the United States. *Five Plays* published.

1965   (March) *Camwood on the Leaves,* a radio play, broadcast on BBC Overseas Service. (September) *The Detainee* (radio play) broadcast on BBC Overseas Service. *Before the Blackout,* satirical revue, produced. (September) *The Road* directed by David Thompson at Theatre Royal, Stratford East, London. (October) Soyinka arrested in connection with a "pirate" broadcast made from the Western Region Studios of the Nigerian Broadcasting Corporation following the disputed Western Region elections. (December) Acquitted.

1965   *The Interpreters* and *The Road* published. *Kongi's Harvest* directed by author at the Federal Palace Hotel, Lagos.

1965-   Senior Lecturer, University of Lagos, and Acting Head of
1967   Department of English.

1966   *Kongi's Harvest* performed at Dakar Festival of Negro Arts. *Rites of the Harmattan Solstice* celebrated at University of Lagos (June 6). (June) *The Trials of Brother Jero* produced at Hampstead Theatre, London. (December) *The Lion and the Jewel* produced at Royal Court Theatre, London.

1967   Awarded the John Whiting Drama Prize. (August) Detained by the Federal Military Government of Nigeria. *Idanre and Other Poems, Kongi's Harvest* published.

1968   Received Jock Campbell *New Statesman* Award. *The Forest of a Thousand Daemons,* Soyinka's translation of D. O. Fagunwa's novel *Ogboju Ode Ninu Igbo Irunmale* published.

1969   (October) Released from detention. Appointed Head of the Department of Theatre Arts, University of Ibadan. *Poems From Prison, Three Short Plays* published.

1970   (August) *Madmen and Specialists* produced at the Eugene O'Neill Theatre Centre, Waterford, Connecticut, United States.

1971   (January) *Madmen and Specialists* performed in Ibadan, Nigeria. *Before the Blackout* published.

CHAPTER 1

Soyinka, the Man and His Background

W OLE Soyinka has his roots in Yoruba culture, as an even
cursory reading of his works soon shows, but his experience extends far wider; his formal education and his working
experience have brought him into contact with ideas from the
whole modern world. This other half of his experience is also
represented in his work. His imagery ranges from tropical yam
roots to the falling acorns of Tegel. But he starts as a Yoruba.

Apart from having been born a Yoruba and thus being naturally a part of the culture, Soyinka has taken a deep and
scholarly interest in the culture of his people. His interest in the
language is strikingly illustrated by his thoughtful translation of
one of the most popular works of Yoruba literature, D. O. Fagunwa's *Ogbodu Ode Ninu Igbo Irunmale* under the title *The
Forest of a Thousand Daemons*. In a very significant Translator's
Note prefixed to the work, Soyinka demonstrates the linguistic
discretion he had to exercise. His explanation of his choice of
the word *daemon* is illustrative of the point. He writes: "The
spelling is important. These beings who inhabit Fagunwa's world
demand at all costs and by every conceivable translator's trick
to be preserved from the common or misleading associations
which substitutes such as *demons, devils* or *gods* evoke in the
reader's mind. At the same time, it is necessary that they trans-
mit the reality of their existence by the same unquestioning
impact and vitality which is conveyed by Fagunwa in the
original."[1] Some of the results of the translator's ingenuity are
new words like *Ghommids, dewild, Gnom* (without an *e*) and
kobold. It is worth noting that these beings from Yoruba tradition found in Fagunwa's world (and in the forests of Tutuola)
are also found in Soyinka's own forests in his play *A Dance Of
The Forests*. The Crier's summons in that play is:

> To all such as dwell in these Forests; Rock devils,
> Earth imps, Tree demons, ghommids, dewilds, genie

Incubi, succubi, windhorls, bits and halves and such
Sons and subjects of Forest Father, and all
That dwell in his domain. . . .[2]

Soyinka shares in this respect the same mythological world as
Fagunwa and Tutuola.

His scholarly interest in this world is further demonstrated
in his essay "The Fourth Stage"[3] in which he develops a theory
of Yoruba tragedy by examining the ideas underlying the Yoruba
concepts of being, and, in particular, the ideas underlying Yoruba
theology. The effect of this deep scholarly interest in Yoruba
culture endows Soyinka with a base of ideas from which his
works flow. Indeed, some knowledge of Yoruba culture is necessary for any serious study of this author's work.

I *Yoruba Culture*

The Yoruba are one of Africa's most remarkable peoples. Their
culture is not only rich but shows a remarkable capacity for
survival in areas far removed from its original home. Yoruba
culture survives robustly, for example, in Brazil and in other
parts of South America, the Caribbean, and in Sierra Leone,
areas which centuries ago, largely through the slave trade, came
into contact with Yoruba of the diaspora.

The original home of the Yoruba is of course Western Nigeria.
G. J. Afolabi Ojo, himself a distinguished Yoruba scholar, defines
their cultural area thus: "the area where Yoruba culture is typical
coincides with the six western provinces of Western Nigeria
[Oyo, Ibadan, Abeokuta, Ijebu, Ondo, Lagos]; Ilorin Division
of Ilorin Province; and Kabba Division of Kabba Province."[4]
Soyinka was born in Abeokuta, an area which still retains the
highest density of Yoruba speakers—over 90 percent of the population, according to Ojo.

II *Gods, Spirits, Ancestors*

Traditional Yoruba life is dominated by religion. The Yoruba
are surrounded by gods and spirits with whom the lives of
mortals interact. In what is more an idiomatic expression
for the idea of multiplicity than an actual head count, the Yoruba
ascribe to themselves four hundred and one gods. (Soyinka prefers to translate a similar expression, *Irunmale*, not literally as

four hundred deities but as "a thousand one one."[5]) The total count of deities probably can never be given since local areas have some deities peculiar to them. There are, of course, major deities who are recognized and worshiped all over Yorubaland. Olodumare (Olorun) is the supreme god—"Creator, King, Omnipotent, All-wise, All-knowing, Judge, Immortal, Invisible and Holy."[6] He is worshiped through minor deities, and although constantly invoked in oaths, the Yoruba do not represent him physically or build shrines to him. In deference to Yoruba tradition (and because he would not know what he looked like anyway), Kola, the artist in Soyinka's novel *The Interpreters,* does not represent Olodumare in his painting of the Yoruba Pantheon. (He appears as Forest Father in *A Dance Of The Forests.*) The gods represented in Kola's canvas are Orisa'Nla, the principal deity under Olodumare; Esu, the spirit of disorder, evil, and change; Sango, god of lightning and electricity; Sopona (Obaluwaiye), god of smallpox; Erinle; Esumare; and Soyinka's favorite god, Ogun. The duality of Ogun's nature, the seeming contradiction in his nature—he is both the creative and the destructive essence—makes him an enigmatic symbol in both Soyinka's own creative work and his criticism. Man in his capacity for both creation and destruction is a reincarnation of this contradictory god of the forge. In "The Fourth Stage," for example, Soyinka writes thus about Ogun:

As for Ogun, he is best understood in Hellenic values as a totality of the Dionysian, Apollonian and Promethean values. Nor is this all. Transcending even today, the distorted myths of his terrorist reputation, traditional poetry records him as "protector of orphans," "roof over the homeless," "terrible guardian of the sacred oath"; Ogun stands in fact for a transcendental humane but rigidly restorative justice.[7]

Below the deities, in Yoruba belief, are numerous spirits of the ancestor and of things. Some of the gods in fact are ancestors who have been elevated into deities. Thus, Sango was once the third Alafin (king) of Oyo. Gods and the spirits of the ancestors are thus very close to each other. Trees, peculiar land formations, rivers, and so on, all could become imbued with spirits which make them sacred. Human life itself is regarded as part of a continuum of life stretching from the spirits of unborn children through bodily existence to the spirits of departed ancestors. The Abiku child who appears as a symbol at the end of *A Dance of the Forests* and is also the subject of a poem is a manifestation of a restless child spirit who is constantly shuttling back and forth between the land of the unborn spirits and this life, causing itself to be born over and over again by the same mother only to plague her by its death. These are the gods and spirits which make up the teeming population of Soyinka's forests in *A Dance of the Forests*.

The ancestors are worshiped through the *egungun,* masked figures who, if the ceremonies are duly observed, become possessed by the spirits they represent and are able to speak with unearthly wisdom. Soyinka makes use of this idea of possession in both *Dance* and *The Road,* two of his most imporant plays. The carving of masks and other objects for the worship of these numerous ancestors and deities has made the Yoruba probably the most prolific as well as the most artistic wood-carvers in the world. A good impression of both their skill and sheer output (it must be remembered that the light wood used is highly perishable, necessitating constant replacement) can be gained from Ulli Beier's illustrated booklet, *The Story of Sacred Wood Carvings from One Small Yoruba Town.*[8] The carver is central to Yoruba life and worship; this central position is reflected in the symbolic role of Demoke, the carver in *Dance of the Forests* who becomes a representative of humanity.

III   *Yoruba Occupations and Festivals*

Farming is the most important occupation of the Yoruba although quite interestingly they are also an urban people, their farms being situated a long way from their homes. Hunting, fishing, weaving, dyeing, and trading are other occupations, but it is the regular rhythm of farming—clearing the farm, hoeing it, sowing it, and reaping the harvest—which dictates the larger patterns of life. A failure of crops is a disaster of the greatest magnitude. In Soyinka's symbolism such a failure becomes a symbol for destruction and the very negation of life, while the image of a successful and plenteous harvest represents the positive forces of life. The big Yoruba festivals predominantly come at the time of harvest when there is plenty to eat and drink. Harvest thus has associations of both piety and joy as is reflected in Soyinka's poem "Idanre."

Some trees and crops have come to be prominent in the culture and assume symbolic stature. Dr. Ojo lists among these yam, kola, oil palm, and maleguetta pepper. These appear in this symbolic role in Soyinka's works; indeed, all of them appear in a single poem, "Dedication." Palm wine, one of the products of the oil palm, is the universal drink; it is a thirst quencher as well as a drink of ceremony and celebration. Tutuola's most famous character, the Drinkard, undertakes his perilous pilgrimage to the land of the dead in pursuit of his dead palm wine tapster without whose services life was insupportable. Palm wine assumes almost a mystical role in Soyinka's work. It is the wine of the Professor's special version of the rite of communion in *The Road*. Egbo has to have a gourd of the best palm wine on his visit with the unnamed girl to his shrine in *The Interpreters*. Soyinka's special interest in palm wine (artistic and gastronomic) is exemplified by a celebration of the rites of the Harmattan solstice which he organized at the university of Lagos and for which he composed poems both in Yoruba and English, all around the theme of palm wine.[9]

Yoruba culture is rich in ceremonies, ranging from the simple ceremonies of regular worship (the principal deities are worshiped every four days) through family ceremonies associated with birth, marriage, death, to the big annual festivals of particular gods, and special ceremonies relating to the crowning and the rule of Obas (kings). Ulli Beier in his booklet *A Year of Sacred Festivals in One Yoruba Town*[10] describes with pictures eleven of the major festivals celebrated in this town of six thousand inhabitants. His list is limited to the big town festivals and does not include the more numerous smaller family and personal celebrations.

The principal external features of these festivals are drumming, singing, dancing, feasting, and sacrifice. Poetic praise songs (*oriki*) and prayers are recited, mimetic dances reenact events whose originals are lost in mythological gloom, sacrifices, often of freshly killed animals are offered, and pent-up spirits are released in general dancing. Oyin Ogunba has pointed out how the Yoruba festival has influenced Soyinka's plays:

But by far the most significant traditional element in these plays is the overall design of a festival. This is particularly true of the plays, namely, *Kongi's Harvest*, *The Strong Breed* and *A Dance of the*

Forests. In each of these plays, the prevailing mood is that of the preparation for or celebration of a great event which produces so much excitement or tension in the whole populace that everybody thinks of nothing but the great event. This is, in fact, the atmosphere that prevails when important ceremonies are performed in traditional Africa and Soyinka in these plays very often catches the essence of the festival mood with the drumming, bustle and other manifestations of a holiday.[11]

The head of Yoruba government is the Oba. He is a king who rules surrounded by ceremony, and he combines both political and priestly functions. The Oba's spiritual authority is exemplified in *Kongi's Harvest* in which, even when the Oba's political authority has been eroded by the new regime of Kongi, he still has reserves of moral and spiritual authority with which to compel deference from the functionaries of the new regime. Baroka, the wily Bale of Ilujinle, is another of Soyinka's evocations of the Yoruba traditional ruler.

All Yoruba culture is enshrined in the language, a highly tonal and musical language which gives the impression of being chanted rather than spoken. These rhythmic and tonal qualities do not come over into English, which is a very different language. What does flow over into Soyinka's English is the wealth of imagery and proverbial formulas which he uses with remarkable effect. Soyinka thinks in images, and his poems in particular are elaborate formulations of imagery which only reveal their full meaning when the image safe is cracked.

IV *Christian Influences*

His Yoruba traditional background provides the key to one part of Soyinka, but it is well to remember that there are other influences as well, so universal that they cannot be so easily identified. Although Soyinka received his basic education up to university level in Nigeria, the content of this education was essentially Christian-European. He has declared that he is no longer a practicing Christian,[12] but the influence of Christianity on his work is quite apparent. He has a facility of biblical reference whch could only come of years of early Bible study. A complete list of biblical references in Soyinka's work would be impressive, but only a few illustrations are given here.

In *The Interpreters*, Dehinwa who deliberately slams the door to aggravate Sagoe's already splitting headache becomes Jael (Judg. 4:21) who drove a nail through Sisera's temples with a tent pin. In the same novel, Joe Golder, dissatisfied with his complexion (being too light for a Negro) felt "like Esau cheated of my birthright," a reference to the well-known story of Esau and Jacob (Gen. 27:36). The life of Christ must have made a deep impression, for there are Christ figures throughout Soyinka's work, often with verbal links with the Bible. "The Dreamer" is an obvious example. He hangs

> Higher than trees a cryptic crown
> Lord of the rebel three
> Thorns lay on a sleep of down
> And myrrh; a mesh
> Of nails, of flesh
> And words that flowered free.

This picture obviously derives from Christ on the cross.[13] There are parallels too between Eman in *The Strong Breed* and Christ. Both men were victims of people for whom they worked, and each died high on a sacred tree leaving the people stunned by their deaths.[14] Willing sacrifice is one of Soyinka's recurrent themes.

The miracle of the feeding of the five thousand (Mark 6) is ironically recalled in the last section of the poem "Ikeja, Friday, Four O'clock" in the words: "Let nought be wasted, gather up for the recurrent session/ Loaves of lead, lusting in the sun's recession." There are undertones of Christ's entry into Jerusalem in "Easter." Some of the references are so natural that they could even be unconscious. Quite obviously, like Dehinwa, Sagoe, and Egbo in *The Interpreters* Soyinka had large doses of Sunday school.

V *Other Influences*

Soyinka's higher education, started at Ibadan, was continued at Leeds where he read English. The Leeds syllabus is very wide in scope and must have brought Soyinka into contact with the whole range of modern European and American Literature. He was one of G. Wilson Knight's memorable pupils. The great literary critic, in his preface to *The Golden Labyrinth*, acknowledges his debt to Soyinka's interpretation of the character of King Lear which in turn influenced his conception of the work. The

English poet Thomas Blackburn, after whom Soyinka wrote his poem "By Little Loving," was another Leeds contact. Describing his other experiences in Britain and continental Europe Soyinka himself said: "I worked in a night-club partly as a barman and partly as a bouncer. During one of the long vacations, I worked as a bricklayer in Holland. Then I taught in a variety of schools in Britain. From very good grammar schools to those which qualify to be called borstals."[15]

Perhaps even more significant was Soyinka's attachment to the Royal Court Theatre, the home of the English Stage Society, where he was a play reader. Some of his early pieces were tried out there; for example, "The Invention" and excerpts from other works formed the program at the Sunday night productions of that theater on November 1, 1959. The attachment to the Royal Court put him in contact with the work of the avant-garde European playwrights as well as with the work of traditional dramatists. (English reviewers of his plays have seen influences on his work ranging from Ben Jonson, through Wycherley, Ibsen, and Chekhov, to Wesker and Pinter.) Soyinka has traveled widely since over a vast area of the world, and, being a sensitive man, has no doubt been influenced. His work is, however, a truly original manifestation of his whole vast range of experience. Certainly this range of experience has given him a worldwide view of mankind, even though he naturally chooses to treat man mainly through the African environment.

Soyinka, however, is primarily an African writer. Whatever influence his work has on the rest of the world—he is now performed in Britain, continental Europe, and America—his primary audience is in Africa. His works should be read and performed a great deal more there than they are. Among the plays, the shorter works, particularly the comedies, are performed fairly often, but the major plays far too seldom. The main reason for this is that the major plays do make considerable demands on the skill of actors and the ingenuity of directors, and tropical Africa does not have professional companies which can put on the plays with the degree of professional skill that they require.

VI Soyinka and the Stage

Soyinka himself is conscious of the need for companies which would keep a body of players long enough together under expert direction so that they could develop the necessary skills for the production of the new African drama which draws on African traditional methods of presentation as well as on the techniques of European and other traditions of theater. On his return from England he formed "The 1960 Masks," the company which put on *A Dance of the Forests* in Nigeria's independence year. Later he formed Orisun Theatre. His hope for permanent theater groups is still far from fulfillment, but as head of the School of Drama at Ibadan University he does have the opportunity of training the right kind of actor.

Soyinka is himself a skilled actor and director whose productions of his own plays demonstrate the fact that a professional production is not necessarily an elaborate production. He directed the premiere of *Kongi's Harvest* on the floor of the conference hall of the Federal Palace Hotel in Lagos without benefit of a proper stage; but, by expert lighting and the sensitive use of music and movement, he created an excellent production. Not every director is a Soyinka, and it must be admitted that plays like *A Dance of the Forests* present formidable problems of staging.

Soyinka's other work, particularly the poetry, has the reputation of being difficult. What this really means is that it demands close and sensitive reading—as does his novel, *The Interpreters.* Very few writers, however, repay this attention more copiously than Soyinka does. However complex he may be, though, it seems ludicrous that in Africa reading lists which contain T. S. Eliot's poetry with its background of classical European mythology and mysticism, should exclude Soyinka on grounds of difficulty.

VII *Basic Concerns*

Soyinka's life is inseparable from his work, much of which arises from a passionate, almost desperate, concern for his society. This concern is apparent in his poetry, drama, and essays, but is not merely literary. It shows itself in his letters to the Nigerian papers which can always be relied upon to rouse enthusiastic support or bitter opposition. Indeed it is this very concern, and the speed with which he translates ideas into action, that puts him so often at odds with institutions and governments. His dramatic resignation from the University of Ife, the celebrated radio station episode, and his detention during most of the

Nigerian Civil War are all examples of Soyinka in uncomfortably exposed positions as a result of deeply held convictions. And yet, Soyinka constantly insists that he is not a "committed" writer. All that this really means, as he explains in the *Spear* interview, is that he is "not committed to any ideology." There can be few writers who believe more deeply in freedom and are prepared to sacrifice as much for it. In his own words:

I believe there is no reason why human beings should not enjoy maximum freedom. In living together in society, we agree to lose some of our freedom. To detract from the maximum freedom socially possible, to me, is treacherous. I do not believe in dictatorship benevolent or malevolent.[16]

It is from deeply held convictions like these that the "works," both literary and social, flow. Soyinka is a unified personality; the artist and the man are one.

The essential ideas which emerge from a reading of Soyinka's work are not specially African ideas, although his characters and their mannerisms are African. His concern is with man on earth. Man is dressed for the nonce in African dress and lives in the sun and the tropical forest, but he represents the whole race. The duality of man's personality, his simultaneous capacity for creation and destruction which makes him almost at every moment a potential victim of his own ingenuity, is a universal trait of homo sapiens who has been given by his creator the gift of free will. In *A Dance of the Forest,* theYoruba-style deity, Forest Father, represents the creator, and Demoke the Yoruba carver represents man. Any universal god or any abstraction for the source of life could take Forest Father's place just as any man of sensibility could take the place of the Yoruba artist.

VIII   *Salvation and the Individual Will*

Soyinka sees society as being in continual need of salvation from itself. This act of salvation is not a mass act; it comes about through the vision and dedication of individuals who doggedly pursue their vision in spite of the opposition of the very society they seek to save. They frequently end up as the victims of the society which benefits from their vision. The salvation of the society, then, depends on the exercise of the individual will. Thus the act of Atunda, the Yoruba slave who fragmented the unified essence and produced many individual essences or gods, is celebrated in "Idanre" as are other individual deities or inspired men (prophets) who by the exercise of their individual will transformed the lives of men. The Yoruba figure then is paralleled by figures from all universal religions. Atunda is a symbol for a universal idea which Yoruba mythology and religion conveniently supplies.

If the individual will is so important, society must make it possible for it to be exercised freely. For Soyinka any form of political repression is a suppression of this individual will, which is the force through which new ideas and new life proceed. The suppression of the individual will is thus a suppression of the very forces of life. This is the point of the play *Kongi's Harvest,* to give just one prominent example of the theme. This is not a Yoruba or an African idea. If it has validity, it is a general validity. The clash between the individual and the society which Soyinka so often portrays in African terms is a universal phenomenon; the martyr who is the positive product of the clash is also fortunately (I reproduce Soyinka's irony) universal.

IX *Concern for Life*

Soyinka's work celebrates life and deprecates its opposite. This opposite includes minor internal repressions, but it also embraces the general wastefulness of war. This is an aspect of Soyinka's work that is most obviously relevant to the whole modern world. Again he finds Yoruba mythology handy with the enveloping images. Ogun, temporarily maddened by drink and indiscriminately killing friend and foe, is a personalization of the idea of the senseless waste that war brings. The message of "Idanre" is a universal one, equally applicable (only more so) to those who are armed with nuclear weapons and to those who have only swords.

A minor variation on the destruction of human potential is man's destruction of the environment. This is a theme—pollution—which has become popular in recent years in the industrialized world. In many parts of Africa it still seems remote. Indeed Africa is at the stage when it is actually clamoring for the factors of pollution as fast as it can obtain them. In one of his earliest plays (and funniest, so that the point is often missed) Soyinka gives the "backward" Oba of Ilujinle a plea for the environment:

And the wish of one old man is
That here and there,
Among the bridges and the murderous roads,
Below the humming birds which
Smoke the face of Sango, dispenser of
The snake-tongued lightning; between this moment
And the reckless broom that will be wielded
In these years to come, we must leave
Virgin plots of lives, rich decay
And the tang of vapour rising from
Forgotten heaps of compost, lying
Undisturbed. . . .[17]

Human life represents constant challenges and constant choices, and man has to thread his way through all the contradictory alternatives. Soyinka himself seems to prefer the personality of Ogun who has always lived a life amidst the challenges and the risks of wrong choices. Ogun (unlike the eternal penitent Obatala who forbids wine to his worshipers), "in proud acceptance of the need to create a challenge for the constant exercise of will and control, enjoins the liberal joy of wine."[18] It is in response to the challenges that man moves toward true wisdom, battered and bruised by his experiences. This is the kind of pilgrimage through all life's opportunities and hazards that Soyinka gives the young interpreters in his novel. These are the kinds of huge concerns which remain in the mind when the particular mannerisms through which they are expressed in individual works have been forgotten. These are the sort of ideas which give Wole Soyinka his universal appeal.

CHAPTER 2

Plays

I   The Swamp Dwellers

THE SWAMP DWELLERS had its first performance in London in 1959 and that same year featured with *The Lion And The Jewel* in a double bill at the Arts Theatre in Ibadan. In a writing span which covers a little over a dozen years, this could be called an early Soyinka play. Although its tone is graver than that of its near contemporary, *The Lion and the Jewel* (it too has its share of humor), it is, like the lighter play, an examination of a society in a state of change.

For such a short play, *The Swamp Dwellers* covers a remarkable range of themes. The village in the swamps which is the setting of the play seems to be poised on the edge of change. It had survived within its strictly sanctioned borders without much threat from outside influences, but now these outside influences have begun to make steady encroachments so that a point of near crisis has been reached. The drain of the youth away to the city no less than the predatory swamps threatens the continued existence of the village. Soyinka infuses into the play a sense of physical danger which reflects the precarious state of the society. Its youth has been vanishing into the city—into the unknown—with a suddenness and a finality which is well pictured in Alu's concern for the safety of his second son, Igwezu, who has stayed out too long on his visit to his ruined farm:

I'm going after him. I don't want to lose him too. I don't want him missing his foothold and vanishing without a cry, without a chance for anyone to save him.

☙   ☙   ☙

I'm going out to shout his name until he hears me. I had another son before the mire drew him into the depths. I don't want Igwezu going the same way. (*Five Plays*, p. 161. Further citations in this chapter are to this volume.)

The all-threatening swamp supplies a physical image for spiritual death. For it turns out that Awuchike, who is pictured in the second passage as having been swallowed by the swamps, is not only alive, but is prospering in the city. But for all the contact he has with his home, he might just as well have been swallowed by the swamp: "Awuchike is dead to you and to this house. Let us not raise his ghost." This spiritual death by which the young sever all familial and indeed all human ties with the village and commit themselves to a totally new life in the towns is one of the main threats to the society of the village. It is also a threat to the humanity of the emigrants too, for the city tends to dehumanize them. One has to develop new ways—a city heart—in order to survive in the city.

Although Awuchike does not appear in person in the play, his shadow is always evident. There is an implicit comparison of him with his less successful brother throughout the play. Sometimes it comes out explicitly as in this exchange between Igwezu and his father: "Father. Tell me, father, is my brother a better man than I?" / "No son. His heart is only more suited to the city" (p. 192). Awuchike has buried himself in the city and has sacrificed the responsibilities of family ties for success in the city. Igwezu, on the other hand, is always looking back to the village—to his parents, and to his farm which for him represented the last prop when all else failed. His first act as soon as he has made a little money in the city is to send his father a barber's chair which he had promised him when he left home—"He's a man for keeping his word" (p. 176). He has religiously performed all the sacrifices required by the Priest of the Serpent, he keeps his mask in the village—a concrete symbol of his spiritual attachment—indeed is a model son and citizen. Yet he meets with humiliating failure in the city and a spiritually more devastating failure when he returns home and finds his farm totally destroyed by the floods. But Awuchike, who has "died" to his roots, has become a very successful timber merchant in the city. This is one of the ironies of the play.

This total failure does inevitably raise questions in Igwezu's mind. In order to articulate these questions, however, he has to have help from outside. This is the role which the blind beggar from the North fulfills in the play. He introduces a completely new force, a new way of thinking into the hidebound society of the village. He comes from the dry North into the flood-prone

riverine swamps. He comes from a different religious tradition—
he is a Moslem—and is therefore not inhibited by the religious
taboos of the village. He has come from such a tradition of
barrenness, has seen such total frustration of his own hopes,
that almost anything offered a chance of hope. In his unshakable
faith in the face of adversity, the beggar shows a spiritual
superiority to Igwezu, which qualifies him to be Igwezu's
mentor. Although the beggar is a Moslem, he is another of
Soyinka's Christ figures. Soyinka's work contains many biblical
references, but few are more pointed than the tableau in this
play in which Alu washes and anoints the feet of the beggar:
"*Alu squats and washes his feet. When this is finished, she wipes
them dry, takes a small jar from one of the shelves, and rubs his
feet with some form of ointment.*" This vividly recalls the washing of Jesus' feet described in Luke 8:37-50. The beggar is also
Christlike in that he enters a hidebound traditional society and
makes men begin to think again. He gives himself selflessly and
unasked for the good of others: "How have I deserved so much
of you that you would beg for me?" (p. 196).

This play is sometimes seen as a rebellion or at least a questioning of tradition by the young—this element is certainly there—
but the influence of the not-so-young beggar from outside the
society should not be minimized. That he is a threat to the established order is seen in the unspoken antagonism between himself
and the pillar of the old order—the Kadiye. At the mention of
"Allah" in the beggar's greeting, the stage directions require
the Kadiye to be "*startled*" (p. 175). He recognizes the threat
from another religion immediately. His mechanical gift of money
is wordlessly spurned by the beggar who "turns his bowl upside
down" when the Kadiye's servant offers to drop a coin into it.
There is indeed a contrast between the representatives of the
two religions which reflects adversely on the Kadiye. The man
from the North is ascetic and abstemious, while the village
priest lives by the fleshpots. The physical contrast is required to
be shown on the stage:

*The blind man is tall and straight. It is obvious from his dress that
he is a stranger to these parts. He wears a long tubular gown, white,
which comes below his calf, and a little skull cap. Down one ear
hangs a fairly large ear-ring, and he wears a thick ring on one of
his fingers. He has a small beard, which, with the skull cap, accentu-*

ates the length of his face and emphasizes its ebony-carving nature.
(p. 168)

The Kadiye is a dramatic contrast:

a big, voluminous creature of about fifty, smooth-faced except for little tufts of beard around his chin. . . . He is bare above the waist. At least half the Kadiye's fingers are ringed. He is followed by a servant, who brushes the flies off him with a horsetail flick.

The grossness of the Kadiye's figure in the midst of a disastrous harvest is an index of his lack of concern for the fate of his flock. The beggar whose perceptions are keener in compensation for his blindness, senses his size from his voice. He asks Igwezu (the question is a teaser which further stimulates Igwezu's doubts about the role of the priest):

> Is he fat, master? When he spoke I detected a certain
> bulk in his voice.
Igwezu: Ay, he is fat. He rolls himself like a fat and greasy
> porpoise. (p. 184)

The beggar's contempt for the Kadiye is already affecting Igwezu—the contempt is obvious in the porpoise simile.

The beggar then is a threat to the hitherto unquestioned role of the Kadiye. But the beggar is not just a mischievous sower of discontent; his history is one of extraordinary fortitude in the face of disaster. His march from the North is itself epic. He has not only overcome his blindness but has liberated himself from his own tradition, which made begging the only occupation open to the blind. This blind man is looking for work, and the insistence with which the man demands it startles Makuri. The beggar has credentials of a moral and spiritual nature which qualify him to raise questions about more complacent regimes.

So intertwined are religion with all life in the village that this questioning comes close to blasphemy. The beggar's startling ideas on land reclamation constitute, in traditional thinking, an invasion of the territory of the Serpent. Such words are "profanities" as the horrified Makuri points out. He explains:

The land that we till and live on has been ours from the beginning of time. The bounds are marked by ageless iroko trees and have lived since the birth of the Serpent, since the birth of the world, since the start of time itself. What is ours is ours. But what belongs to the Serpent may never be taken from him. (pp. 173-74)

It is obvious from Makuri's reaction that he and his generation are totally unreceptive to new ideas. They have achieved a resigned compromise with their surroundings, a fatalistic acceptance of good and evil which is a kind of peace. They seem to be the last for whom the village would give that total security and happiness to which they look back in their reminiscences early in the play. If there is to be change, then it has to come from somewhere else. His double failure in spite of all his efforts makes the youthful ear of Igwezu more receptive to the beggar's influence. Makuri's attitude is interesting because there are occasional signs that he too has doubts about both Priest and Serpent. His near blasphemy may have been an unconscious slip brought on by Alu's perversity: "The serpent be ... Bah! you'll make me voice a sacrilege before I can stay my tongue" (p. 162). His pique at the Kadiye's slights loosens his tongue a little more, and he calls the revered Kadiye (behind his back of course) "The pot-bellied pig" (179). He is not, however, ready to question any further, and contents himself with such occasional mutterings.

The relationship between the beggar and Igwezu is central to the play. Igwezu's entrance for his meeting with the beggar is well timed (the entrances and exits in this play are beautifully organized so that they become thematically significant). From the very opening of the play, the dialogue prepares for Igwezu's entrance. When he does appear, he comes in unobserved by the others at a crucial point in the beggar's narration of his last disappointment—a ruined harvest. This is thematically apt. Igwezu has just returned from viewing and contemplating a similar catastrophe. Makuri in an earlier speech indicates the extent of Igwezu's disaster: "Not a grain was saved, not one tuber in the soil. ... And what the flood left behind was poisoned by the oil in the swamp water. ... It is hard for him, coming back for a harvest that isn't there" (p. 173). It is a total disaster, but not unprecedented. The beggar—he is blind to boot—has suffered with his people in a similar disappointment in the dry North, and it is the narration of this disaster that Igwezu, unseen, hears. The beggar's tale is particularly poignant because the expected harvest seemed to have brought a new humanity to the village. The disaster was therefore a defeat, not only for their bodies, but for their very souls:

Nothing could keep us from the farms from the moment that the shoots came through the surface, and all through the months of waiting. We went round the plantains and rubbed our skins lightly against them, lightly, so that the tenderest bud could not be hurt. This was the closest that we had ever felt to one another. This was the moment that the village became a clan, and the clan a household, and even that was taken by Allah in one of his large hands and kneaded together with the clay of the earth. We loved the sound of a man's passing footsteps as if the rustle of his breath it was that gave life to the sprouting wonder around us. We even forgot to beg, and lived on the marvel of this new birth of the land, and the rich smell of its goodness. . . . But it turned out to have been an act of spite. The feast was not meant for us,—but for the locusts. (pp. 181-82)

Igwezu hears not only this but also the beggar's resolute response to this total collapse of his hopes: "I headed away from my home, and set foot towards the river." For the beggar, the man from the dry North, water was life. He was spiritually thirsty for water—any kind of water: "But let there be water, because I am sick of the dryness." Water had been the cause of Igwezu's ruin—the very water for which the blind man craved.

The beggar's narration establishes his credentials in Igwezu's mind, although he has yet to relive his disaster and come to terms with himself. He too has had a bitter "feast" (the beggar too uses the word "feast" somewhat ironically in his narration): "I have had my feast of welcome. I found it on the farm where the beans and the corn had made an everlasting pottage with the mud" (p. 183). When the beggar makes the surprisingly hopeful proposal, he arouses a new interest in Igwezu who looks up at him "as if seeing him for the first time" (p. 184). Once the beggar catches Igwezu's attention he plies him with questions, the answers to which would make all the difference between Igwezu's continued acceptance of the old ways of living and some attempt to discover new paths. He repeats, for example, to a more hopeful ear his earlier question about the obstacles in the way of a new approach to the land: "Do you serve the Serpent, master? Do you believe with the old man—that the land may not be redeemed? That the rotting swamps may not be purified?" (p. 185). He prods more sensitive areas—the well-fed priest and, glancingly, the god himself—"Does the priest live well? Is the Serpent well kept and nourished?" (p. 185). Receiving the right sort of response, he moves directly at the god: "How does the Serpent fare in times of dearth? Does he thrive on the poisonous crabs? Does he drink the ooze of the mire?" This is too much for Makuri, who interrupts this dangerous line of questioning—"that borders on sacrilege" (p. 186). The beggar's work is half done, however. He retires gracefully and hands the role of questioner neatly to Igwezu: "It is for the master to question, not the slave." How well the beggar had done his work is seen in the encounter between Igwezu and the priest when for once the latter loses his superior position and lies helpless in the barber's chair looking up at the razor in Igwezu's hand.

When Igwezu challenges the priest and subjects him (in the manner of the beggar) to a series of searching questions, he is challenging the whole conservative basis of life in the village by which the Kadiye, acting on behalf of the Serpent, sets the bounds of human conduct, and swallows their offerings with little regard to their fates. All his contempt for the Kadiye's venality comes out in his question: "Why are you so fat, Kadiye?" The priest stands exposed as a false prophet. There is no mistaking the pun on "lie" in Igwezu's verdict on the priest: "You lie upon the land, Kadiye, and choke it in the folds of a serpent" (p. 195). Igwezu has emancipated himself mentally through his questions from the tyranny of the Kadiye and the Serpent. He realizes that essentially he is now on his own. This is a hard discovery: "If I slew the fatted calf, Kadiye, do you think the land might breathe again? If I slew all the cattle in the land and sacrificed every measure of goodness, would it make any difference to our lives, Kadiye? Would it make any difference to our fates?" (p. 195). Igwezu's mood is one of despair. He has shaken off the old shackles, but he still has to work out something as positive as the beggar's resolute search for a new life. He himself is bewildered by the newfound strength with which he has challenged the Kadiye. Has it an abiding, positive quality?

I wonder what drove me on

              *   *   *

Do you think that my strength was that of despair? Or was there something of a desire to prove myself? (p. 196)

Igwezu's departure for the city after all this is not a decisive
gesture. He does not see any new hope there. The analogy between the city and the swamp recurs in his despairing question:
"Is it of any earthly use to change one slough for another?"
He has to leave the village because he has challenged the basis
of its existence and "must not be here when the people call for
blood" (p. 197). His departure then is forced and is thus for
the time being a negative reaction. Nor is there any hope in his
words of a return in due course: "Only the children and the old
stay here, bondsman. Only the innocent and the dotards" (p.
197). In this mood there is no hint of a return. But Igwezu has
gone through an experience which has shaken all his old
beliefs, and so when he sets out, it is without the old props
afforded by the Kadiye and the Serpent. The question is whether
he is strong enough to go through life on his own. We do not
know, and he does not know. The beggar watches and waits. "I
shall be here to give account."

In a brilliant arrangement of exits, the beggar is left symbolically alone on the stage. Alu and Makuri—the two dried-up
representatives of the old life—had opened the play, taunting
each other with gibes at their own decrepitude. They are a
failing generation and have symbolically faded from the scene.
The Kadiye, the bastion of the old life, has been shown in a
vulnerable moment, and his venality has been exposed. After
his triumph over the Kadiye, the beggar had called Igwezu
"slayer of Serpents." The Serpent and all he represents has not
been completely slain, but his regime has been shaken for the
first time; it is vulnerable. The discomfited Kadiye would no
doubt organize a temporary rally, a holding operation, but that
regime too will crumble. It would have been easy to see the
young Igwezu completing the rout of the old forces, but Soyinka,
as he does time and time again, shuns such easy solutions. The
forces of tradition are not so easily routed. Igwezu is certainly
not strong enough to oppose the Kadiye—at least not yet—so he
has to flee. Any hope of change within the village is represented
by a blind beggar who is, in spite of his handicap, a spiritually
strong force. He is the only hope in a village of innocents and
dotards. But some seeds once sown have a way of thriving in
the most unpromising surroundings. Sometimes, on the other
hand, they just die. This is the kind of open situation that we
have at the end of The Swamp Dwellers.

II The Lion and the Jewel

The Lion and the Jewel, like *The Swamp Dwellers* is set in an African village which is facing the challenge of rapid change. Soyinka gives a visual image of the state of the village in the opening set which is "dominated by an immense 'odan' tree," with the "bush school" only flanking the stage on the right. The bush school is yet to occupy center stage in village life and cannot yet provide, with its mechanical chanting of the "Arithmetic times," a substitute for the established traditional basis of village life. This is, in fact, the crux of the play: what would happen to the village of Ilujinle if by a kind of magic the Bale and Lakunle were to change places and the latter were able to put his ideas into practice? There is little doubt that the result would be total confusion. Viewed in this way, the play would be seen to be not a contrast between progress and reaction—represented by Lakunle and the Bale—but between a muddle-headed sloganeering and a hard-headed conservatism. Conservatism (it is certainly not held up as an ideal) wins because it has a clearer view of life and, in the prevailing state of the contest, is more likely to succeed. Within the context of the play a victory for Lakunle would have been against the evidence, just as outside the context of the play the results of his confused social leadership would be disastrous.

Lakunle is half-baked where both Sidi and the Bale are sound. The stage directions describe Sidi as *"a true village belle."* "True" is indicative of her genuine quality. *"She balances a pail on her head with accustomed ease. Around her is wrapped the familiar broad cloth which is folded just above the breasts, leaving the shoulders bare."* (This "exposure" causes the self-conscious Lakunle acute embarrassment.) In contrast to Sidi, Lakunle is ridiculous in the costume by which he vainly strives to hold on desperately to the coattails of a fashion he does not understand. His appearance, *"in an old-style English suit, threadbare but not ragged, cleaned but not ironed,"* signals a man of unformed values, incompetently imitative. His words soon confirm the visual image.

Soyinka's portrayal of Lakunle is subtle. He emerges as a comic character, but there is an underlying pathos arising from the recognition that he has a split personality, the two separate halves of which are clearly visible. He is engaged in doing

violence to his "true" nature. Although he loudly denounces the
Bale for his backwardness—chief among the Bale's sins is his
practice of polygamy—Lakunle secretly envies the man just
this. It is with a start that he has to recall himself to his "civilised" duty when his mind wanders off in unconscious admiration
of the Bale. (His true nature sometimes gets the better of him,
and he indulges in a little bottom-pinching himself.) His speech
in criticism of the Bale demonstrates both the real Lakunle which
he tries to suppress and the bloodless substitute which he holds
in front of himself:

> Voluptuous beast! He loves this life too well
> To bear to part from it. And motor roads
> And railways would do just that, forcing
> Civilisation at his door. He foresaw it
> And he barred the gates, securing fast
> His dogs and horses, his wives and all his
> Concubines . . . ah, yes . . . all those concubines
> Baroka has such a selective eye, none suits him
> But the best . . .
> [*His eyes truly light up . . .*]
> . . . Yes, one must grant him that.
> Ah, I sometimes wish I led his kind of life.
> Such luscious bosoms make his nightly pillow.
> I am sure he keeps a time-table just as
> I do at school. Only way to ensure fair play
> I don't know what the women see in him. His eyes
> Are small and always red with wine. He must
> Possess some secret . . . No! I don't envy him!
> Just one woman for me.
> Alone I stand
> For progress, with Sidi as my chosen soul-mate, the one
> Woman of my life. . . .   (p. 117. Further citations
>   in this chapter are to this volume.)

The unresolved split in Lakunle's personality is signaled by a
subtle change in style within the speech. When he slips from
his conscious posturing into an almost subconscious musing,
the playwright eases him into a more natural linguistic register.
"Luscious bosom" is the sort of phrase he shuns in his conscious
posturing. (In his first encounter with Sidi he had had recourse
to the euphemistic "shoulders" as a substitute for breasts:

How often must I tell you, Sidi, that
A grown up girl must cover up her . . .
Her shoulders? I can see quite . . . quite
A good portion of—that!)

During his reverie his guard comes down, and the honestly appreciative phrase "luscious bosoms" comes tumbling out from his smothered soul. The syntax, too, gradually eases up to approximate to normal colloquial speech: "I am sure he keeps a time-table just as I do at school." The comparison with his school timetable is natural and apt. Once he recovers himself, however, and the prudish sentinel takes over, he returns to a rhetorical style studded with the clichés from his book-learning. The inverted syntax signals the return of the respectable veneer: "Alone I stand/ For progress, with Sidi as my chosen soul-mate, the one/ Woman of my life." This is an example of Soyinka's subtle use of linguistic register to highlight Lakunle's total unfitness for the role of reformer with which he flatters himself. An examination of any of his speeches of more than a line or two in length usually reveals a potentially disastrous mental confusion. The ideas which come pouring out are so undigested as to become comic. Even when these ideas have some appearance of worth, the way in which they are presented show that in Lakunle's mind they really have no meaning. Soyinka usually provides the deflating device within the speech itself, so that by the time it is over Lakunle has succeeded in emptying his own ideas of any validity they may have seemed to have.

Lakunle rejects the traditional form of marriage—the bride-price in particular—as "a savage custom." In its place he would put a "civilised" institution. But the very form of address "Ignorant girl"—with which his speech begins—signals both his dangerous conceit and an impetuous lack of control. Phrases like "To buy a heifer off a market stall" (with "heifer" standing out like a sore thumb), "chattel," and the stilted "wed" suggest his books rather than Lakunle himself as the real speaker. As the speech proceeds and Lakunle triumphantly makes each proposition for the wrong reason, he isolates himself from both his society and the sympathy of the audience, so that he becomes an object of ridicule and the butt of his own missiles:

Ignorant girl, can you not understand?
To pay the price would be

> To buy a heifer off the market stall.
> You'd be my chattel, my mere property.
> No, Sidi! [*very tenderly*]
> When we are wed, you shall not walk or sit
> Tethered, as it were, to my dirtied heels. (p. 100)

Even at this stage, and in spite of the danger signals which have been pointed out, the speech still manages only to skirt total disaster. But it continues:

> Together we shall sit at table
> —Not on the floor—and eat,
> Not with fingers, but with knives
> And forks, and breakable plates
> Like civilised beings.

The end of the statement completely destroys any worth the beginning may have had. The proposition that eating off "breakable plates" is civilized is a prime example of Lakunle's thinking. Quite obviously by isolating the most irrelevant and least valuable attribute of a certain type of plate, and using this as the mark of civilization, Lakunle shows that he does not understand anything either about plates or about civilization. The technique of deflation is repeated as the speech continues:

> I will not have you wait on me
> Till I have dined my fill.
> No wife of mine, no lawful wedded wife
> Shall eat the leavings off my plate—
> That is for children.

Apart from the mechanical crib from the prayer book—"lawful wedded wife"—which signals the imitator rather than the reformer, the proposition seems acceptable until Lakunle brings it all crashing down with "That is for children." The resulting proposition is ridiculous, for it becomes something like "Civilized parents feed their children on the leavings of their plate."

Of course, by this point of the play Lakunle's fate is sealed, and no minute examination of his speeches is needed to throw audiences into convulsions of laughter almost every time he opens his mouth. His very appearance, so carefully detailed at the beginning of the play, serves as an ever-present deflating device. When he assumes the weary pose of the prophet crying

out in vain in the wilderness, or of the great man of ideas casting his pearls before swine, the effect is hilarious; that is just
what he is not:

> [*wearily*] It's never any use.
> Bush-girl you are, bush-girl you'll always be;
> Uncivilised and primitive—bush-girl!
> I kissed you as all educated men—
> And Christians—kiss their wives.
> It is the way of civilised romance.   (p. 100)

It is clear, then, that this ridiculous figure does not represent
any kind of progress. (The contrast between him and Eman in
The Strong Breed is total.) He is a self-proclaimed prophet, but
as he himself follows a false trail, he cannot lead his society
anywhere but to disaster.

The Bale is quite different. He is conservative, resists the
building of roads and railways, and tries to keep his society
largely insulated from "progress." If progress is represented by
Lakunle's vapid descriptions of it, then it can be said without
hesitation that the village of Ilujinle would be better off without
it. According to Lakunle, the Bale has deprived the village of
"Trade,/ Progress, adventure, success, civilisation/ Fame, international conspicuousity" (p. 116). (He could have gone on to
itemize cocktail parties, a school of ballroom dancing, a modern
park for lovers, "High-heeled shoes for the lady, red paint/ on
her lips," breakable plates, etc., as he does elsewhere.) All these,
merely for their own sake, Ilujinle could happily do without.

The Bale fears progress, and in this he can be credited with
the foresight of anticipating some of the disasters of progress
which "civilized" societies have only discovered by hindsight.
His statement on progress is a far more controlled utterance than
Lakunle's, and thus has some integrity:

> I do not hate progress, only its nature
> Which makes all roofs and faces look the same.
> And the wish of one old man is
> That here and there,
> Among the bridges and the murderous roads,
> Below the humming birds which
> Smoke the face of Sango, dispenser of
> The snake-tongued lightning; between this moment
> And the reckless broom that will be wielded

In these years to come, we must leave
Virgin plots of lives, rich decay
And the tang of vapour rising from
Forgotten heaps of compost, lying
Undisturbed. . . . (p. 144)

There is wisdom here in that the Bale sees the reverse side of
the coin of progress, which in Soyinka's work is frequently symbolized by the motor road, which not only speeds things up, but
can also be justly described by the Bale's term, "murderous."

Of course, the mere apprehension of danger is not in itself
constructive. The Bale's reaction to progress is conservative
in a negative way. (It must be remembered that in the speech
just quoted the Bale is doing some word-spinning in the process
of subduing Sidi to his will. His own view of himself is therefore most attractively presented. The Bale has made two very
strange concessions to progress. Fascinated by the idea of
postage stamps, he has designed a pathetically inefficient stamp
machine so that Ilujinle "Will boast its own tax on paper, made
with/ Stamps like this. For long I dreamt it/ And here it stands,
child of my thoughts" (p. 142). That this strange machine which
does not work—"All is not well with it"—has the immediate
effect of impressing Sidi with the Bale's ingenuity, should not
blind us to the fact of its total incongruity in an illiterate society.
The Bale has also allowed his servants to form a trade union—
"The Palace Workers Union"—and has conceded them a day off,
"in keeping/ With the habits—I am told—of modern towns." There
is an element of whim in both the Bale's gestures to progress,
rather than any deliberate selection of desirable items from the
package of progress. He is in reality a conservative under whom
the village is likely to remain exactly as it has always been if he
has his way. Even so, he is certainly the lesser of two evils. No
doubt change is inevitable. The village school itself is an index of
this. With the intrusion of the photographer, too, the village is
shown to be vulnerable. The Bale would, in spite of himself, have
to yield to change. He would not, however, have started the slide
himself, and he at least knows what he does not want. He also
has some idea of what he wants for himself, and how to get it.
While Lakunle plies his barren rhetoric and tries vainly to suppress his natural feelings, the Bale enjoys his harem, his wrestling and his favorite delicacy—a mixture of "ground corn and
pepper." The Bale, in short, lives, while Lakunle frustrates his

own vitality. They represent opposing values which in more somber works are equated with the opposed principles of life and death.

The winning of Sidi by the Bale is only logical in the play, since Lakunle's concern is for rhetoric and the Bale's concern is for life. It is clear that Lakunle desires Sidi more with his head than with his heart. He wants to rescue a poor "bush-girl" and "civilise" her with marriage. He must do this on his own terms: "I obey my books. . . ./ Man takes the fallen woman by the hand/ And ever after they live happily" (p. 153). Sidi's feelings and wishes do not enter in the business at all. His is not a wooing; it is a piece of misguided social evangelism.

The Bale, on the other hand, is a past master in the practical arts of wooing, and while Lakunle only succeeds in irritating Sidi, the Bale, once by his strategem—even the worldly-wise Sadiku is completely deceived—he get her into his palace, succeeds in first dazzling the girl, then eventually compelling her admiration. Nor are his intentions merely intellectual, as Sidi soon finds out! The Baroka is as virile as he is wily. By comparison, Lakunle is as trivial and emasculated as Sidi's contemptuous comparison implies:

> I who have felt the strength,
> The perpetual youthful zest
> Of the panther of the trees?
> And would I choose a watered-down,
> A beardless version of unripened man? (p. 155)

There is an interesting side glance in the play at the sex war—the opposition of male and female—which explodes into a victory dance when Sadiku believes that the Bale has become impotent. Up to this point in the play Sadiku has appeared as the ideal head wife in a polygamous household. Not only does she not complain about the institution of polygamy, she is an enthusiastic wooer of new wives for her husband. So totally is she immersed in the system that Sidi's contemptuous rejection of the Bale's offer of marriage, and her very assumption that she has any choice once she is asked, totally scandalizes Sadiku who can only pray for a restoration of Sidi's wits: "May Sango restore your wits. For most surely some angry god has taken possession of you" (p. 115). Sadiku just cannot contemplate the consequences of Sidi's attempt to assert this independent role. It would appear,

however, that under her obedient conformity seethes a basic
resentment against her prescribed role. The Bale's impotence
(or her belief in it) releases her suppressed feelings, and she
invites Sidi to celebrate with her the victory of their sex over
the dominating male:

> Not me alone girl. You too. Every woman. Oh
> my daughter, that I have lived to see this day. . . .
> To see him fizzle with the drabbest puff of a mis-
> primed 'sakabula.'
>> Take warning my masters. . . .
>> We'll scotch you in the end. (p. 125)

So much then for the comfortable male doctrine of the contented,
uncomplaining, compliant female who totally accepts the system
of polygamy. Unfortunately for Sadiku, and even more for Sidi,
the victory celebration is premature. There is still plenty of
life left in the old lion.

The play is a harmonious blend of words, song, dance, and
mime. Soyinka's use of mime and dance in particular is worth
some notice. Twice in the play, once to represent the first visit
of the photographer and again to represent the Bale's bribing of
the railway surveyor, mime and dance are used structurally to
recall past events. This use of the flashback technique, more
commonly associated with the cinema, gives the play historical
depth. In this play the scene for each of these flashbacks is
obviously set, and we know we are being given a glimpse of
the past. In *The Strong Breed* there is an even bolder breaking
up of time divisions so that at moments the play seems to be
suspended in a fusion of past and present. A similar scrambling
of time is seen also in the technique of narration used in *The
Interpreters*.

Because *The Lion and the Jewel* is a comedy, the follies of
Lakunle result only in his own mild discomfiture. He is a false
leader, but fortunately no one follows him. Indeed, the play
ends on a note of hope for Lakunle himself when he seems to
be on the verge of giving his heart a chance as he is seen
fascinated by the buttocks of the dancing girl. One feels that
if he can only let himself really dance wthout being prompted,
he might yet be saved. Other false prophets in Soyinka's works
—the Kadiye in *The Strong Breed*, for example—represent a
more sinister threat to their society.

III A Dance of the Forests

A Dance of the Forests presents a comprehensive view of man over a massive span of history; it even—in the highly symbolic chorussing of the future—looks into the future. For Soyinka, history is a nearly cyclical movement, any progress being represented by a kink after an evolution and at the start of a new cycle. "Idanre" invokes the image of the snake swallowing its own tail and that of the "mobius strip," a figure of interlocking rings, to represent this idea:

> multiform
> Evolution of the self-devouring snake to spatials
> New in symbol, banked loop of the "Mobius Strip"
> And interlock of re-creative rings, one surface
> Yet full comb of angles, uni-plane, yet sensuous with
> Complexities of mind and motion.
>> (*Idanre and Other Poems*, p. 83)

A Dance of the Forests is an attempt to represent the complexities of the human personality and its consequences within this cyclical pattern of history. The result is a very complex play with tremendous possibilities for staging as well as for interpretation; it is a warning against moral complacency and escapism.

The action takes place at a crucial point in the particular evolutionary pattern in which the play is set—the completion of a cycle. Since it was written for Nigeria's independence, the end of an era and the beginning of another, this is apt. The Crier who announces the ceremony of "the welcome of the dead" invites only those of the dead who have completed a cycle:

> only such
> May resume their body corporeal as are summoned
> When the understreams that whirl them endlessly
> Complete a circle. Only such may regain
> Voice auditorial as are summoned when their link
> With the living has fully repeated its nature, has
> Re-impressed fully on the tapestry of Igbehinadun
> In approximate duplicate of actions, be they
> Of good or of evil, of violence or carelessness;
> In approximate duplicate of motives, be they
> Illusory, tangible, commendable, or damnable.
>> (*Five Plays*, p. 50. Further citations in this
>> chapter are to this volume.)

Another cycle has been completed and characters who took part in the cycle represented by the court of Mata Kharibu eight centuries earlier are now present at the beginning of the following cycle, represented at the social level by the "Gathering of the Tribes" (which could be taken to represent independence and the ceremonies celebrating it). At another and more important level, this is also an opportunity for stocktaking, self-examination, self-confession, and possible self-regeneration. While all are involved in the social celebration, only a few human beings—representatives of the race—take part in the process of introspection, and even these represent different levels of feeling and different capacities for understanding what they see. Demoke is obviously far more capable of feeling and understanding than Adenebi, for example.

Although a particular geographical and social setting is selected for what amounts to a trial, it is important to remember that it is not just Nigerian man who is under examination but homo sapiens as a whole. The use of gods and spirits, the backward plunge into history, as well as the peering into the future with the aid of possessed humans, all combine to give the play an archetypal quality and an application broader than any confining parcel of space or time.

Numerous themes appear—some only momentarily—in this vast drama, but they are all contained under a broad enveloping theme of the contradictions of man's nature and the consequences of such contradictions (both as it involves the single man and as it varies from man to man) for the whole race of man and his environment. The environment involves not only other men and trees and rivers and minerals but also gods and the spirits of the dead who act as prodders and stimulators to the human conscience. Within this vast framework there is room for a great variety of subthemes—the nature and functions of art, political corruption, the destruction of the natural environment, war, changes in humane values brought about by "modernisation," the consequences of free will—a profusion of themes which arise naturally from Soyinka's treatment of the overall theme. No wonder then that as Margaret Laurence comments, "There are some parts of *A Dance of the Forests* which seem overloaded. There are moments when the multiplicity of themes creates the feeling that there are a few too many plates spinning in the air—some of them speed by without being properly seen,

and some crash down."[2] Margaret Laurence's own interpretation
of the play is most sensitive and points a path through all these
complexities, thus proving that the play is complex but not confused. Indeed the problems arise mainly over the precise interpretation of the significance of the drama of the Half-Child at
the end. Each succeeding reading produces insights which
suggest a complete vision on the part of the author. It thus
seems very likely that Margaret Laurence's expectations of the
play will be fulfilled, namely that what is obscure to us "may
seem perfectly plain to the next generation of readers and play-
goers."

In addition to the multiplicity of themes, there is a multiplicity of symbols. One of the difficulties of interpretation may
arise not merely from the multiplicity of symbols but from the
use of different symbols to reinforce the same idea. Man is the
central figure in the play, and man is represented by living
men and women—Demoke, Adenebi, Rola, Agboreko, The Old
Man, and so forth. Some of these have a dual existence in that
they also appear as historical characters in the court of Mata
Kharibu. (This device conveniently establishes the essential
continuity of human nature.) The Dead Man and Woman also
represent man—man as victim of other men—and history as an
indictment of man's past actions. The ants also represent man
or rather men—the mass of men who are the victims of those
in power—the manipulated masses. Man is also represented by
the half-child, that ambiguous symbol of man's future. One has
to be prepared for these changing symbols for different aspects
of the same thing and respond to them. A perfectly coherent
interpretation of the play is possible with a little care, though
there will always be questions and disagreements over particular details.

The Gathering of the Tribes, the central social event, is celebrated in the town (sometimes called village), but its sounds
and its effects penetrate into the forest which is the scene of
the spiritual exercise of introspection. At the end of the play,
just after Demoke's crucial restoration of the Half-Child to his
mother, there is a silhouette of rejoicings in the town which
emphasizes the isolation of the social celebration from the deeper
spiritual action which is taking place in the Forest: "*A silhouette
of Demoke's token is seen. The village people dancing round it,
also in silhouette, in silence. There is no contact between them*

and the Forest ones" (p. 82). This tableau underlines one of the themes of the play—the insensitivity of the generality of men to the deeper spiritual concerns, and their preoccupation with the mere externals of life. Here as in other works of Soyinka, it is given to a few—often only to a lonely individual—to seek and find the vision for the community as a whole. This is the opportunity which the play gives to the three human protagonists, Demoke, Rola, and Adenebi. These characters are clearly distinguished from each other, and their differences must be appreciated for a satisfactory interpretation of the play.

Adenebi is the least sensitive of the three. He is a council orator in this life, and in an earlier existence had produced the play's most rhetorical speech in defense of Mata Karibu's indefensible war. (Rhetoric of Adenebi's kind is frequently a mark of insincerity or hollowness in Soyinka's work.) Adenebi is given a thin surface respectability signaled by his rhetoric but also by his consciousness of his social position and his reluctance to be *seen* in the wrong company. When Rola's notorious identity as a prostitute becomes known, his one worry is that he would be contaminated by "scandal": "The whole horrible scandal. How did I ever get in your company?" (p. 25), and more explicitly: "Oh yes, and I found that the woman who was with us was that notorious lady they call Madame Tortoise. That was really why I left. Think, if I, a councillor, was discovered with her!" Underneath this respectable exterior is concealed an involvement with petty municipal corruption exemplified by the "Incinerator" episode.

Adenebi's insensitivity is even more clearly demonstrated by his general lack of taste. In his enthusiasm for a new civilization, he is curiously without firm values. He has forsaken the humane hospitable ways of the past, and he cloaks his lack of humane hospitality under his responsibilities to "a proper family life," "privacy," and so forth. But there is indecision even in his expression of his new creed, signaled here by "I suppose," "you know," and his hesitant delivery: "It is rather difficult. I suppose one has to be firm. You start your own family, expect to look after your wife and children, lead—you know—a proper family life. Privacy . . . very important . . . some measure of privacy" (p. 5).

Adenebi is incapable of appreciating art, his mind having been sealed off by a rule of thumb by which anything "pagan" is bad: "I really ought to tell you how disappointed I was with your son's handiwork. Don't you think it was rather pagan? I should have thought that something more in keeping with our progress would be more appropriate" (p. 33). His whole attitude is one of respectable philistinism. In this spirit he had supported the Old Man's proposal for an invitation to the ancesters to join in the celebration and had enveloped the whole scheme in his characteristic rhetoric. His picture of the ancestors is dangerously romantic: "Purple robes. White horses dressed in gold. Processions through the town with communion and service around our symbol" (p. 33). This shallow insensitive man is Council Orator and, in an earlier existence, Court Historian. In this earlier role he had silenced the common sense of the unwilling Warrior in the flood of rhetoric with which he supported the causeless war of Mata Karibu and branded the Warrior as a traitor (pp. 57-58). In return for a bribe he had testified to the soundness of the slave dealer's boat which he had never seen. Adenebi in both existences represents the insensitive, corrupt, philistine trimmer who is always loud in support of power and of doctrines conducive to his own convenience. He is a clearly delineated person and is at the same time a manifestation of a type.

Rola is an odd mixture. In both existences she is a woman with a fatal attractiveness whose path is littered with dead lovers whom she callously sends to their death. In her current existence, she too has repudiated the traditional ways and finds family hospitality a burden: "This whole family business sickens me. Let everybody lead their own lives" (p. 6). The implied selfishness and lack of humane feeling are given a more sinister expression in her attitude to men whose lives have no value beyond their role as ministers to her own convenience. They are expendable pawns in her business. Her fierce defense of her position carries incidentally an ironic satirical comment on a society which is indifferent to human life in its preoccupation with money-making: "When your business men ruin the lesser ones, do you go crying to them? I also have no pity for the one who invested foolishly. Investors, that is all they ever were—to me" (p. 24). Rola's attitude in an earlier existence had exactly paralleled this one. A rejected lover who committed suicide had been selected, "just as I select a new pin every day. He came back again and could not understand why the door was barred to him. He was such a fool" (p. 64). Rola represents in this side of her nature a destructive force. The Dead Woman excludes her

from womanhood as a source of new life: "I am certain she had
no womb, but I think/ *It* was a woman." (The last pronoun, italics
mine, is significant.)

About all that can be said for Rola in either existence is that
she shows some appreciation of art. She is not quite the philistine
that Adenebi is in this regard. The expression with which she is
to say these lines to Demoke (according to the stage directions)
suggests an awed appreciation of the carver's skill: "[*with unexpected solemnity.*] And you did not even cut it down. Climbing·
the king of trees and carving it as it stood—I think it was very
brave" (p. 7). (It would perhaps be carping to observe that
Rola's admiration is rather more for the carver's daring than for
the resulting work of art.) This quality in Rola would not have
been worth mentioning, had not art and the appreciation of
art as an index of moral sensitiveness been so important in
Soyinka's work. The words of Obaneji (who is really Forest
Head—the chief of the gods) in appreciation of Demoke's art
are significant, particularly since his speech is a rejoinder to
Rola's own remark last quoted: "It is the kind of action that
redeems mankind."

Because of this sensitivity, the significance of the ceremony
of the welcome of the dead is not entirely lost on Rola. She comes
out of the experience looking (in the words of the stage directions) "*chastened.*" And Demoke (she herself is too overawed
to speak)· yokes her with him in the experience. She is no longer
what she had been, the heartless "Madame Tortoise": "Not any
more. It was the same lightning that seared us through the
head" (p. 85). (It is significant that Adenebi just fades out of
the play, being incapable of any response to the vision he has
just seen.) Rola/Madame Tortoise is rather more complex than
appears on the surface. She is certainly capable of redemption
and is thus nearer to the most sensitive of the three human protagonists, Demoke.

Demoke is the artist. (The redemptive role of art and the
artist in Soyinka's work has been remarked on before.) In his
earlier existence—as the Court Poet—he had also lived as an
artist. Yet he too involves a contradiction. Being human, even
this extraordinary artist is susceptible to jealousy and vertigo;
he is capable of destruction as well as creation; of murder as
well as the production of an extraordinary work of art—"the
kind of action that redeems mankind." In the scenes showing

his earlier existence, his work as a poet is not highlighted—
except in the fulsome poetic phrases with which he praises
Madame Tortoise—but his dual nature is even there suggested
by the contrast between the deep contempt (revealed in asides),
which he feels at Madame Tortoise's callousness, and the flattery
which he lavishes on her in her hearing: "Your hair is the feathers
my lady, and the breast of the canary—your forehead my lady—
is the inspiraton of your servant. Madame, you must not say
you have lost your canary—[*aside*] unless it be your virtue,
slut" (p. 52). He is bold enough to defy Madame Tortoise and
forbid his novice to go on the hazardous errand to recover the
canary—"I forbid him to go" (p. 53)—and his innuendos almost
bring down the wrath of his callous mistress on his head: "And
look out my poet; sometimes, you grow wearisome" (p. 67).[3]
But it is Demoke the carver (not the earlier Court Poet) who has
the greater significance for the play.

Demoke combines the destructive and the creative capabilities
of man. His very act of creation involves destruction. The majestic *araba* has to be destroyed in order to produce the totem. This
is a necessary act, however, and a limited one. The further
destruction of the forest by the townspeople, and the resulting
vulgarization of his work, disgusts Demoke: "When I finished
it, the grove was cleared of all the other trees, the bush was razed
and a motor road built right up to it. It looked different. It was
no longer my work. I fled from it" (p. 8). Unlike the destruction
of the araba tree, the murder of Oremole is not necessary; it is
a crime, and the memory of it plagues Demoke's soul until he
confesses it. At first he skirts round his crime. He mentions the
death of his apprentice as though it had nothing to do with him:
"And one man fell to his death" (p. 7). The growing uneasiness
of his conscience is dramatized by his compulsive urge to question the dead—he is the only one of the protagonists who takes
any real interest in them. But what begins as an anxiety that his
crime might be revealed by the voices of the dead, becomes—
with the help of the Forest Head's gentle prodding—an irre-
sistible urge to make an open confession. This leaves the way
open for the regeneration, which is Forest Head's purpose in
ordering the welcome ceremony. Sokinka dramatizes the murder
in a verbal flashback heightened by poetry. The narration high-
lights the mixture of jealousy and humiliation which motivated

Demoke to murder his apprentice because he could climb higher
than his master:

> I plucked him down.
> Demoke's head is no woman's cloth, spread
> To receive wood shavings from a carpenter.
> Down, down I plucked him, screaming on Oro. (pp. 27-28)

This act of murder is immediately succeeded by a frenzied
act of creation no less vividly described:

> Before he made hard obeisance to his earth,
> My axe was executioner at Oro's neck. Alone,
> Alone I cut the strands that mocked me, till head
> And boastful slave lay side by side, and I
> Demoke, sat on the shoulders of the tree, . . .
> My spirit set free and singing, my hands
> My father's hands possessed by demons of blood
> And I carved three days and nights till tools
> Were blunted, and these hands, my father's hands
> Swelled big as tree trunk.

Both acts—of destruction and creation—are essentially Demoke's,
in spite of Ogun's attempts to take over the responsibilities of
his protégé's crime: "In all that he did he followed my bidding.
I will speak for him" (p. 66).

Demoke's open confession of his crime (as well as a triumphant assertion of his act of creation) is in contrast to the reactions
of both Adenebi and Rola to the proddings of Forest Head.
Adenebi, for ever shoring up the façade of respectability which
covers his real nature, never admits anything. We can only
deduce his complicity in municipal corruption. He staves off the
questions of Obaneji (Forest Head) with a show of sensitive
anger (p. 17). He is equally furious at the same questioner's
attempt to get him to say what sort of death he would like to
die. (The answers of both Rola and Demoke are self-revelatory.)
Adenebi misses the opportunity of self-examination and confession offered by Forest Head and hence disqualifies himself
from benefiting from the significance of the welcome of the dead.

Rola's reaction is different again. Once pushed to the corner,
she fiercely turns against her accusers. (It is significant that
Adenebi baits her mercilessly—"What! No shame. No shame
at all" [p. 22] while Demoke is almost protective.) Indeed she
seems at one point to lay the blame for her conduct on her nature:

"I owe all that happened to my nature." But she also admits her own responsibility in a defiant, satisfied way: "I only know I am master of my fate. I have turned my training to good account. I am wealthy, and I know where my wealth comes from" (p. 24). There is some honesty here which is totally absent from Adenebi's hypocritical reactions. Rola could thus take some meaning from the vision at the end. These, then, are the three living human protagonists who witness the welcome of the dead.

The dead, variously called by uneasy human beings "accusers," "executioners," and other derogatory names have been invited by Aroni to trouble the conscience of the living. Their appearance does have this effect. Demoke's father is the most concerned to drive them back. He wants to keep the part of the past which these dead represent, hidden. To him in particular they bring memories of his son's crime which he would not have revealed. But he really speaks for men in general when he says that these particular dead "have come to undermine our strength. To preach to us how ignoble we are." The Old Man is here resisting the truth about himself and the rest of mankind; he is denying his true history and his true nature. It was he and Adenebi who had put the proposal to the Council to invite representatives of the ancestors as guests at the Gathering, but they wanted only guests who would flatter their ideas of themselves. They wanted only the noble, not the ignoble side of their history and their nature represented. "We were sent the wrong people. We asked for statesmen and were sent executioners" (p. 30). And "If we can drive them away from here, it will be sufficient" (p. 29).

This refusal to face the fact that man is capable of both creation and destruction, of both nobility and meanness, and the consequent failure to take this into good account in national thinking, constitute a dangerous romanticism. It makes men totally unprepared when the results of this other side—the evil side—of their natures suddenly overtakes them. For Soyinka even outside this play, Africans (particularly writers) who indulge in this kind of myth-making are lulling their people into a dangerously false sense of virtue out of which a sudden discovery of their own viciousness rudely wakes them and finds them unprepared:

We, whose humanity the poets celebrated before the proof, whose lyric innocence was daily questioned by the pages of the newspapers, are now being forced by disaster, not foresight, to a reconsideration of our relationship with the outer world. It seems that the time has

now come when the African writer must have the courage to determine what alone can be salvaged from the recurrent cycle of human
stupidity.

The myth of irrational nobility, of a racial essence that must come
to the rescue of the white depravity, has run its full course. It never
in fact existed, for this was not the problem but the camouflage.[4]

The Old Man in trying to hunt the Dead Man and Woman
away from earth, to smoke them out with petrol fumes, is involved
in a game of "camouflage"—of smothering the truth under a pall
of smoke. Fortunately the Old Man's son, Demoke, acknowledges
the presence of the dead and, through this, acknowledges the
duality of man's nature so that (as apparently happened to him
when he murdered his apprentice) man's viciousness will not
take him by surprise. Unfortunately for most men it is the
camouflage, the racial myth, that is important. Conscience and
the unpleasant parts of the truth, represented by the dead,
must be suppressed. Eventually the truth comes out; the
ancestors cannot be so easily got rid of, and the Old Man's
efforts prove futile. As the Elder Agboreko asks: "Will you never
believe that you cannot get rid of ancestors with the toys of
children . . . ?" (p. 41).

The historical section of the play, the Court of Mata Kharibu,
is an evocation of the truth of the past. Such a court had been
in the mind of the Old Man and Adenebi when they made their
proposal for the invitation—'Mali, Songhai. Perhaps a descendant
of the great Lisabi Zimbabwe. Maybe the legendary Prester
John himself . . . I was thinking of heroes like they" (p. 33).
The court shown in the play has the external trappings of what
Adenebi wanted. Mata Kharibu is powerful and keeps a glitter-
ing court, but he is also vicious. He is surrounded by learned
men, but they do not have the courage to speak the truth. The
one man in the court who has the courage to speak the truth is
emasculated and sold as a eunuch. The court scene is beautifully
balanced, with the brutal tyranny of Mata Kharibu on one side
of the stage complemented by the coquettish cruelty of Madame
Tortoise on the other. The results are the same—the condemnation
of human beings to death in fulfillment of a whim. Both violate
the sanctity of human life for trivial purposes. The Court contained not only prostituted academics and distinguished bribe-
takers but also that sinister figure (usually pictured as an alien
but here pictured as one of the nation) the slave dealer—a man

who thrives on the miseries of others. All the characters are recognizable in our own times. Soyinka underlines this by giving the Historian, the Poet, and Madame Tortoise a contemporary existence, as well as by bringing the dead man and woman from this court into the contemporary world to witness against the living.

The whole play moves toward the "welcome of the dead" which Aroni has organized on behalf of Forest Father. This is the real climax. The earlier sections prepare the minds of the mortal characters for the experience and inexorably draw all the participants to the scene of welcome.

The human characters have been looked at, but a glance at some of the Forest dwellers—the gods—is necessary. Forest Father is the supreme deity, the creator who has endowed man with free will, and now has to endure the pain of watching his creation perversely choosing the wrong path over and over again. Interfering would be to deny man his free will, and Forest Head will not do this. All he can do is every so often—at the completion of a cycle—to give man an opportunity of looking into his real self, to "pierce the encrustations of soul-deadening habit, and bare the mirror of original nakedness—knowing full well, it is all futility" (p. 82). It is to this end that the welcome ceremony is staged.

Aroni, who acts on behalf of Forest Father and who like an Elizabethan "Presenter" gives a prologue to the play, is an embodiment of wisdom and justice. His role, then, is to bring men to justice and make public what is hidden. In the words of Agboreko: "Aroni is Wisdom itself. When he means to expose the weaknesses of human lives, there is nothing can stop him. And he knows how to choose his time" (pp. 34-35). Agboreko's reference to "the scales of Aroni" (p. 35) emphasizes his judicial role. He does not, however, pass judgment. He only "exposes" the evidence in the hope that the right self-verdict will be given by man himself. "Let the future judge them by reversal of its path or by stubborn continuation" (p. 67).

Ogun and Eshuoro, although Forest Dwellers (gods), are curiously linked to men, not only by the fact that they are respectively patrons of Demoke and Oremole, but also by their humanlike conduct. Forest Father, who has to come between them as they spring at each other's throats, comments: "Soon, I will not tell you from the humans,/ So closely have their habits

grown on you" (p. 67). They are contrasted one with the other,
but they are also shown (as are the human beings) as embodying
contradictions within themselves. (It is probably wise to take
these two beings as they are defined within the play rather than
to bring too much from external knowledge of the Yoruba
Pantheon. In any case, Eshuoro is a special creation for the play
of a combination of two deities Eshu and Oro.) The two
deities are introduced by Aroni in his opening "testimony":

Eshuoro is the wayward flesh of Oro—Oro whose agency serves much
of the bestial human, whom they invoke for terror. Ogun, they
deify, for his playground is the battlefield, but he loves the anvil
and protects all carvers, smiths, and all workers in metal. (p. 2)

Eshuoro (also described in the list of characters as a wayward
cult-spirit) comes out in the play as an enemy of man, particularly of the noble part of man's nature. His attitude to Demoke's
totem seems to bear this out. He is unable to see the work of art;
he is so obsessed with the desecration of his tree and the insult
to his dignity that this implies:

The totem, my final insult. The final taunt from the human pigs.
The tree that is marked down for Oro, the tree from which my
follower fell to his death. . . . But my body was stripped by the
impious hands of Demoke, Ogun's favoured slave of the forge. My
head was hacked off by his axe. Trampled on, bled on, my body's
shame pointed at the sky by the edge of Demoke, will I let this day
pass without vengeance claimed blood for sap? (pp. 47-48)

This is the voice of pique. Eshuoro's anger seems to spread over
all men—"the human pigs"—and transcends the single act of
Demoke. It is as a general enemy of man that he functions in
the final pageant of the play. His inability to see the work of
art reminds us of the philistinism of Adenebi. Murete is in-
furiated by Eshuoro's attitude to the totem, and his speech points
to the place of art in Forest Father's scheme of things:

that is an offering which would have gladdened the heart of Forest
Father himself. He would have called it adulation. Did he not
himself teach them the arts, and must they be confined to little
rotted chips which fall off when Eshuoro peels like a snake of the
previous year . . . ?

This restores the balance. For Eshuoro appears as something of the protector of the Forest. He quite rightly resents the indiscriminate deforestation and pollution which have taken place: "Have you seen how much of the forest has been torn down for their petty decorations?" (p. 45) and "The whole forest stinks. Stinks of human obscenities" (p. 46). (Indiscriminate deforestation is often a signal of human vandalism—in *The Lion and the Jewel*, for example.) In extending his wrath to the totem and condemning it, however, Eshuoro shows a lack of discrimination and taste. He acts out of mere pique and ruins his case. In any event, his pique leads him to work his rage out on Murete's tree, thus neutralizing somewhat his role as protector of the Forest (pp. 44-45). Eshuoro also seems to be incapable of seeing the heroism of the Warrior's conduct: "The soldier was a fool. A woman. He was a woman" (p. 65). He obviously preferred the bloodthirsty self-destructive path of man. His general malevolence to man is seen even more clearly in the final dance.

Ogun is prominent in the play as the god of creativity and of art. He is Demoke's patron and champion, defending everything Demoke does and accepting responsibility for his crime. "I, Ogun, swear that his hands were mine in every action of his life" (p. 67). This is of course an excessive claim as Forest Head's rejoinder implies. But it at least establishes his complicity in and condonation of the crime. He too like his protégé combines both the elements of creativity and destruction—"His playground is the battle-field" as well as the studio. He and Demoke seem to be on the same side of the struggle for the Half-Child at the end. He is thus identified with man in the struggle against the merely bestial, which Eshuoro represents.

These qualities of the gods are important in an interpretation of the complex dance which is the climax of the play. From the very opening of the play attention is directed to a trial at the end. The dead man and woman come out of the ground looking for human advocates to take their "case." It soon becomes clear that a trial is to be organized by Forest Head: "Forest Father, masquerading as a human,/ Bringing them to judgment" (p. 29). The nature of this judgment is further revealed as a process of self-judgment and self-condemnation to be undertaken by the human beings themselves. It is Aroni's purpose "To let the living condemn themselves" (p. 37). Later Forest Father himself gives out that he has summoned the welcoming "for ends of my own"

(p. 67) which in the words of Aroni are to give man an opportunity for regeneration. "It is enough that they discover their own regeneration." The particular cases of the dead man and woman become involved with a more general case involving all mankind. It is ironical that at first the dead man and woman look to Demoke to take their case until they discover that he too is on trial. "What is this? The one who was to take my case—has he sent another down? Into the pit?" (p. 26).

The hearing of the particular cases of the dead man and woman become mixed up in the general trial at the end. In the more general case of man which soon emerges, the dead woman speaks not just for herself. Her question is "For all the rest":

> Say someone comes
> For all the rest. Say someone asks—
> Was it for this, for this,
> Children plagued their mothers?

The question suggests a consciousness of the ultimate futility of human life. Was it worth it all? In her particular case—she is accused of depriving her unborn child of life by herself committing suicide—she pleads weakness. She did not see the point of continuing either her own or the child's life. She had in fact tried to save the child the futility of life. But this is wrong. The suffering cannot be escaped as Forest Head points out: "Child, there is no choice but one of suffering." This point having been established, interest shifts from the woman to the dead man. His appearance establishes that all his three existences (the other two are not indicated) have entailed unjustified suffering, and like the dead woman he wants rest: "I have come to sleep" (p. 70). The Questioner (Eshuoro in disguise) accuses him of having learned nothing. He had let power (in the Court of Mata Kharibu) slip through his fingers. He is to be condemned to wander a hundred years more. Eshuoro is merely repeating his earlier opinion, which encourages man's degeneracy. At this inconclusive stage of his particular case, the dead man is ushered off and never appears again. The two particular cases seem to be dropped but the dead woman features prominently in the drama of the Half-Child later.

A new drama is introduced when the three human protagonists are masked and become possessed so that they speak, not in their own voices, but for the various spirits who now appear. Into this drama is woven the drama of the Half-Child, the details of which have caused readers of this play the most trouble.[5] The chorus of the spirits by comparison is fairly straightforward. The spirits together symbolize the total environment of Africa—all its resources and all its potentialities. To what purpose will they all be used? The suggestions are that they will be used unwisely, even destructively. The spirit of the palm whose sap is ordinarily life-giving—it "suckles"—will turn to blood, because of the evil in man's nature—"blackened hearts."

> White skeins wove me, I, Spirit of the Palm
> Now course I red.
> I who suckle blackened hearts, know
> Heads will fall down
> Crimson in their bed!

The imagery indicates a violation of the processes of life, a contamination of the sources of nourishment for life. (Soyinka frequently portrays this idea through images of an aborted harvest.) Each spirit speaks in a similar vein showing man doomed through a perverse exploitation of his resources. The pollution of the sources of life so that they become the sources of death is clearly imaged in the chorus of the waters:

> Let no man lave his feet
> In any stream, in any lake
> In rapids or in cataracts
> Let no woman think to bake
> Her cornmeal wrapped in leaves
> With water gathered of the rain
> He'll think his eye deceives
> Who treads the ripples where I run
> In shallows   (pp. 69-70)

The Half-Child too joins in the chorus of a doomed future: "I'll be born dead/ I'll be born dead."

The Ants, representing the masses who are exploited by their leaders (they had been mischievously persuaded to come to the trial by Eshuoro) picture their enslaved and exploited state: "We are the ever legion of the world/ Smitten, for—'the good to come'" (p. 78). The facile political morality of leaders is given dramatic form in the distorted triplets. They are physical manifestations of the rhetorical distortions which are used to justify political crimes: "I am the Greater Cause, standing ever ready/ Excusing the crimes of today for tomorrow's mirage." The satire on human perversiy is obvious in passages like these; the significance of these symbols is not obscure.

The Half-Child, it has been suggested earlier, is a symbol of man's future. That this future is doomed is clear in the Half-Child's chorus, "I'll be born dead." But Soyinka involves him in a further tableau whose significance is less clear. He engages (against his will) in a game of *sesan* with Figure in Red (who turns out to be Eshuoro) and loses. His life is thus forfeited to the bestial Eshuoro. But Eshuoro is not allowed to carry off his prize. Ogun intervenes. We recall here the contrast between the natures of Ogun and Eshuoro and read into his act some sort of salvation for the child. The fate of the Half-Child is for some time in the balance with Eshuoro and his jester trying to win him to one side, while his mother, Demoke, and Ogun all seem to fight on the same side for its possession. These forces are the natural mother (though this is complicated in that this one is dead), the artist representing the noble side of man's nature, and the god of creativity. The peril of the Half-Child is vividly dramatized in the dance in which it is tossed between Eshuoro, the third triplet (posterity) and Eshuoro's jester while Demoke tries to rescue it from the obvious peril represented by the knives.[6] It is Ogun, however, who intervenes, rescues the child, and passes him to Demoke. Here the symbolism is so thick that one can only make suggestions for an interpretation.

Demoke, having rescued the child, stands confused. Although the mother had originally wanted to be relieved of her burden and leave the living child with the living ("I said the living would save me" [p. 20] and "I thought . . . here was a chance to return the living to the living that I may sleep lighter" [p. 5]), at this point she seems to have changed her mind and wants the child back—she mutely appeals to Demoke for the child (p. 82). Demoke apparently cannot in any case be allowed to keep the child because his keeping it would in some way "reverse the deed that was begun many lives ago." Therefore, "the Forest will not let you" (p. 82). Demoke's act would somehow have broken the cycle. Now this would have been clear had the dilemma been Ogun's—if, for example, he had hesitated between keeping the child under his own protection and hence interfering, or giving the child to Demoke as a representative of the living thus leaving man with his free will. He does not hesitate, however, and hands the child to Demoke. What then is the significance of Demoke's dilemma and his handing the child to the dead woman, who presumably returns with it to the world of the dead (for ever? Can he be born again?). At this point even the suggestion that the Half-Child is a symbol of man's future begins to look weak.

Leaving aside intransigent details, the general point seems to be that Forest Father will not intervene; man is returned to his own kind and the exercise of his free will with the risk that he will continue to frustrate his own happiness. The cycle continues as before.

This whole pageant has been laid on for the benefit of the human protagonists. They pass through fire, and the effect on Demoke is traumatic. Although three human beings witness the welcome, only two appear afterward. Adenebi fades out—not surprisingly, perhaps, because of his insensitive nature. But only the most insensitive can come through the vision unchanged. Demoke suggests that they will never be the same again: "We three who lived many lives in this one night, have we not done enough? Have we not felt enough for the memory of our remaining lives?" (p. 85). Certainly Madame Tortoise is not the same. That she survives alive surprises Agboreko: "I did not think to find her still alive." She now seems regenerated—"chastened"—having been seared by the same "lightning" as Demoke. The effect of the experience on Adenebi, the least sensitive of the three, is not stressed, but only the most insensitive could come through such a vision completely unaffected.

While there are people capable of undergoing the spiritual experience of total introspection, of piercing "the encrustations of soul-deadening habit" which is represented by the participation in the welcome ceremony, there is presumably some hope for man's regeneration. Ogun's rescue of Demoke when he falls from the totem seems to reinforce this possibility of hope. Even so, this is not certain. (It is significant that the human beings are compelled by Forest Father to face the truth about themselves in this way.) The general picture which emerges from the play is that of man ruthlessly exploiting his natural environment and other men for his own limited, selfish ends; of man so preoccupied with his material concerns that he neglects matters of the spirit, growing progressively insensitive. The play suggests

the need for an occasional pause for thought—in the case of
Nigeria what better time than the occasion of independence
and the start of a new cycle? On such occasions instead of a
total absorption in the externals of celebration, instead of white-
washing our history and true nature in pageants of splendor, men
should face the truth, the whole truth about themselves, and
with a mixture of hope and trepidation move into the uncertain
future.

A *Dance of the Forests* has all the ingredients for a spectacular
play, but only in the most capable hands. A bad production would
be an unmitigated disaster. The set has to suggest the timeless
element of the play, particularly in the welcome scene when the
stage directions require a setting suggestive of a meeting point of
existences. The dark wet atmosphere suggests the "dark backward and abysm" of time—the scene of the beginnings of amoebal
life—while the "rotting wood" and "mounds" suggest an apoc-
alyptic scene of death and the end of life. This re-creation
would require all the ingenuity of the technician:

*Back-scene lights up gradually to reveal a dark, wet, atmosphere
dripping moisture, and soft, moist soil. A palm tree sways at a low
angle, broken but still alive. Seemingly lightning reduced stumps.
Rotting wood all over the ground. A mound or two here and there.*

This unearthly scene is necessary to convey the out-of-time
atmosphere of the last section of the play. The Mata Kharibu
section has to be differently lit again from the here-and-now
scenes in the forest.

The costuming too gives opportunity for spectacular designs
which should at the same time clearly distinguish the characters
one from another and remind the audience of their identities
when they appear either in disguise or in different historical
periods. It would probably be helpful during Aroni's "testimony,"
which introduces the main lines of the play, if the characters
appear on the stage in a tableau as they are named. The ironies
implicit in Forest Father's exchanges with the human characters
would be immediately appreciated by the audience if he had
already been introduced and seen as Forest Father disguised as
Obaneji during Aroni's "testimony." The final tableau with spirits
of things (whose distinctive natures would have to be suggested
by their costumes), masked human beings, a Half-Child, the
grotesque triplets, ants, gods, all describing their own movement

patterns, would make either a spectacular scene or total confusion. The hazards of staging aptly reflect the hazards of interpreting this grandly complex play.

IV   The Strong Breed

The Strong Breed is an extraordinarily compact play. In spite of its comparative brevity it is one of Soyinka's most significant works in which one of the playwright's constant preoccupations—the need for sacrifice—is dramatized. It is also one of Soyinka's most symbolic plays. (*Camwood on the Leaves*, an unpublished radio play, is more obviously symbolic but lacks the subtlety of this play.) It avoids cluttering detail and thus succeeds in presenting its themes in an archetypal form. Evil, for example, about which the play is so concerned—the evil of the village which has to be expiated—is never defined although it hovers over the whole play like a pall. The effect of this avoidance of definition is to give the play a generality of application. Sacrifice, too, which Eman represents is treated symbolically. The "carrier," obviously in the case of the effigy, but also in the case of Eman-as-carrier, is a symbol for the moral force required to save the society.

Eman's sacrifice is modeled on the sacrifice of Christ, whose death is recalled by a number of subtle references. Like Christ, Eman is both teacher and healer. This is economically dramatized before even the first words of the play are spoken. (Soyinka's stage directions are almost always significant, but the opening ones particularly so, for they often have symbolic significance.) When the play opens, "*Sunma is clearing the table of what looks like a modest clinic. . . . Another rough table in the room is piled with exercise books, two or three worn text-books etc*" (*Five Plays*, p. 287. Further citations in this chapter are to this volume.) The suggestions of this opening tableau are dramatized later in Eman's painful efforts at helping in the rehabilitation of the helpless idiot Ifada, as well as in his kindness to the inscrutable girl who, Judas-like, betrays him. Eman eventually goes on to carry the evil of the village on his own head. The parallel with Christ continues in that Eman works among people who neither understand nor really want him. As Sunma complains, "You are wasting your life on people who really want you out of the way" (224). Other analogies with Christ are Eman's conscious sacrifice of himself for an ungrateful people, his supreme sacrifice taking the form of his being hanged on a sacred tree. Toward the climax of the physical sacrifice, his body flinches, and he needs water. Eman's pathetic appeal to the girl who betrays him parallels Christ's agonized cry, "I thirst." Eman's death, like Christ's, stuns the people in whose name it had been demanded and leaves a remarkable impression on some unlikely minds. There is no dramatic parallel to the dying thief, but one of the elders of the village, Oroge, suddenly pauses at a crucial stage of the pursuit of Eman because he has caught a reflection of something in the victim's face which impresses him: "He saw something. Why may I not know what it was?" (262). This influence at his death is also reflected in the inability of the villagers "to raise a curse"—the traditional curse with which each man is expected to empty his evil on the victim. The analogies with Christ also link Eman with Soyinka's crucified figure in his poem "The Dreamer," which is examined elsewhere in this book (pp. 117-19). Eman, then, within the play is the savior.

In consonance with the archetypal nature of the play, the evil against which Eman works is not treated in detail. It is nevertheless potently symbolized. It is an opposite force to what Eman himself represents. He is sensitive to human need regardless of kinship, while in the tradition of the village, outsiders are fair game. It is easy to see here a symbolic treatment of that ethnic exclusiveness, tribalism, which so bedevils life in modern Africa, but the applications are even wider. Eman represents a responsiveness to human need wherever it arises. He himself is a "stranger" in a village where the plight of the stranger, particularly on the eve of the new year, is a fearful one. An early tableau dramatizes this: *Two villagers, obvious travelers, pass hurriedly in front of the house . . . the man enters first, turns and urges the woman who is just emerging to hurry* (p. 237). The reason for the anxiety of the travelers to escape from the hostile village becomes clear as the play develops. Sunma, an insider who has become disgusted with the village and seeks to escape from it, refers to the tribal exclusiveness in one of her appeals to Eman to leave: "Have you not noticed how tightly we shut out strangers? Even if you lived here for a lifetime, you would remain a stranger" (p. 247). But the attitude of the village to strangers goes further. A stranger is required to bear the evils of the village, a task none of the villagers has the moral strength to undertake. Their seeming kindness to outsiders like the help-less Ifada is shown to be a mere device for recruiting victims:

Oroge: No one in his right senses would do such a job. Why do you think we give refuge to idiots like him? We don't know where he came from. One morning, he is simply there, just like that. From nowhere at all. You see, there is a purpose in that. (p. 254)

Ifada thus becomes a prime candidate for the ordeal of "carrier." To Eman this is appalling—"But why do you pick on a helpless boy? Obviously he is not willing" (p. 253). He has been brought up in a different tradition: "In my home, we believe that a man should be willing" (p. 253). There is a confrontation of values here which leads directly to Eman's substitution of himself for Ifada, and his assumption of the role of the willing carrier of the evils of the village, a decision which leads to his martyrdom. Eman's humanity is in contrast to the brutal callousness of the village. He is a moral force without which the village would remain unregenerate in spite of the ritual of an annual sacrifice.

If Eman is the symbol of a humane response to need, the inscrutable girl symbolizes the attitudes of the village. She is curiously detached and is totally unaffected by human need. The stage directions make the following requirements of the actress: *"The girl is unsmiling. She possesses in fact, a kind of inscrutabil-ity which does not make her hard but is unsettling"* (p. 240). Her sickness also isolates her from the rest of the village—a fact she states without much discomposure: "I am unwell you know. . . . Don't you know I play alone? The other children won't come near me. Their mothers would beat them" (p. 241). Typically in the play the precise nature of her illness is not stated. It merely isolates her and, in her mother's hope, will disappear, borne away by her carrier with the old year (p. 241). It is significant that she does not seek medical help for the illness and refuses to go near Eman, who runs a free clinic. Her sickness seems to be another symbol for archetypal evil. To Sunma, "She is not a child. She is as evil as the rest of them" (p. 242). All her actions confirm her as cold-blooded and selfish, characteristics she shares with the rest of the village.

In the symbolism of the play, her carrier also represents Eman; this effigy is tortured and eventually hanged to represent his fate. Given the child's identification with the village, this use of her carrier is most appropriate and saves the play from a distracting concern with the details of Eman's agony, which could have reduced tragedy to melodrama. The girl of course proves to be a Judas and callously betrays Eman when at the end of the play he asks her for water, and instead of giving it to him she reveals his hiding place to his pursuers.

The girl's callousness is manifested particularly in her relations with Ifada, whom she merely uses because he is all that is available. Ifada is the play's symbol of need, a need which makes no more impression on the girl than it does on the village she represents. To her, Ifada is a despicable object for which, however, because of her isolation she has some need. This reflects exactly the boy's position in the village as a whole. The girl's invitation to play comes at the end of a callous inventory: "[*after a long, cool survey of Ifada*] You have a head like a spider's egg, and your mouth dribbles like a roof. But there is no one else. Would you like to play?" (p. 242).

Sunma is a member of the village, but one who moves in the play from consciousness of the evil of the village and a desire to escape from it, to an open renunciation of its evil. Such renunciation totally isolates her from the protection of the village, thus putting her in line for a path which might, like Eman's, lead to a life of further sacrifice. Sunma's concern throughout most of the play is that she and Eman should escape from a village that has come to revolt her. Obviously, she has come under his influence and is inclined to his way of life. It is she who is seen clearing away the tools of Eman's trade in the opening tableau of the play. What she lacks is Eman's extraordinary strength which enables him to keep his composure in the face of evil. She has to get away from it:

> I wonder if I really sprang from here. I know they are evil and I am not. From the oldest to the smallest child, they are nourished in evil and unwholesomeness in which I have no part
>
> *   *   *
>
> But you must help me tear myself away from here. (p. 242)

In her consciousness of evil and her instinctive desire to run away from something she has come to hate, Sunma is a good, humane person, but unlike Eman, an *ordinarily* good, humane person. She lacks the strength of an *exceptionally* good, humane, person such as Eman is. (Eman is after all one of the Strong Breed—an exceptional breed as the play makes clear.) She had in fact run away once before, but had bravely returned to help Eman in his work (p. 244). Eman is thus a prop to her weak humanity. Without her strong attachment to him, she would have left the village and its needs for ever. At the opening of the play she is poised once again on a moment of decision: "Eman, are we going or aren't we? You will leave it till too late" (p. 237). And again: "It is the time for making changes in one's life" (p. 245). Eman will not leave, and as the sounds of the departing lorry symbolize, the moment of decision passes, and she stays on with Eman in his battle with evil. She is thus forced to remain and continue to face the evil of the village. Already in her heart she had renounced this evil, but her open renunciation was to come later in the confrontation with her father.

Sunma's attempts at escape are of a piece with her sudden fierce hostility toward Ifada at the beginning of the play. This too is an attempt at escape. She after all had seemed to be as responsive to Ifada's need as Eman, who is consequently surprised at her sudden outbursts against the boy. After one of her expressions of disgust—"horrible insect"—Eman cannot conceal his surprise: "I don't understand. It is *Ifada* you know. Ifada! the unfortunate one who runs errands for you and doesn't hurt a soul" (p. 238). Sunma's frustration at Eman's refusal to leave finds an outlet in the symbol of the need which keeps him tied to the village. Indeed as Eman points out, "It is almost as if you are forcing yourself to hate him. Why?" (p. 240). Sunma is trying another break from her responsibility; she is trying to escape into hatred from love—the responsibilities of love make much greater demands than those of hate. Her decision to stay by Eman has committed her to a path, the full consequences of which appear later. She reinforces her mental renunciation of the evil of the village with a physical confrontation with her father in which the antipathy of their conflicting attitudes is externally dramatized. Sunma attacks her father savagely, drawing blood. The symbolic struggle is brief but intense:

[*Jaguna turns just in time to see Sunma fly at him, clawing at his face like a caged tigress.*]

Sunma: Murderer! What are you doing to him. Murderer! Murderer!

[*Jaguna finds himself struggling really hard to keep off his daughter, he succeeds in pushing her off and striking her so hard on the face that she falls to her knees. He moves on her to hit her again.*]

Oroge: [*comes between*] Think what you are doing Jaguna, she is
          your daughter.
Jaguna: My daughter! Does this one look like my daughter? Let me
          cripple the harlot for life . . .
          [*Draws his hand across his cheek—it is covered with
          blood.*] (pp. 262-63)

This is Sunma's final break with the society. It is true that this
open confrontation is stimulated by her personal concern for the
fate of Eman who at this point is being pursued as the victim,
but it is no less of a conscious break with evil for all that. It is an
evil which she had mentally renounced much earlier anyway.
Whatever the reasons, her actions have now made her an
outsider.

Sunma's social isolation is dramatized by her new relationship with Ifada. She had tried earlier to reject him, identifying
him with the cause of her frustration. Now, after the break with
Jaguna, she accepts him as rescuer, comforter, and friend. The
tableau required by the stage directions after the fight between
father and daughter dramatizes the new relationship: "*Ifada,
who came in with Sunma and had stood apart, horror-stricken,
comes shyly forward. He helps Sunma up. They go off, he holding
Sunma bent and sobbing*" (p. 263). Later too they are united
by their common feelings at the sight of the hanging effigy, which
represents the martyred Eman. Their feelings are in contrast to
the reactions of the girl who stands "impassively watching," as
detached from any contact with the human situation as she has
always been.

The role of Eman in the play has been incidentally demonstrated in the examination of the other characters, since he is
central to the play. He represents a moral force which transcends
social boundaries. His is the broad humanity which the world
both needs and rejects at the same time, while individuals and
individual societies relentlessly pursue their particular concerns.
But Eman is also a man. As a son and a pupil, he has relations
with a father and his tutor. As a lover and husband he suffers
the agony of losing his wife. He is human enough to prefer a
quiet life to a life of self-sacrifice, but eventually an inner urge
which he is unable to resist drives him on to accept the burden
of sacrifice. He cannot escape this role because he is of the
Strong Breed.

Through the concept of the Strong Breed Soyinka makes the

point that the quality of personal leadership through suffering is not a common characteristic. It is rare. This is well symbolized in the notion of the carrier. The role carries with it a tremendous moral burden at which strong men flinch. It involves a moral preparedness which is implied in these words of Eman's father as he prepares to carry the evils of his own village: "A man should be at his strongest when he takes the boat my friend. To be weighed down inside and out is not a wise thing. I hope when the moment comes I shall have found my strength!" (p. 259). Such is the weight of the burden that the men of Jaguna's village have to foist the role on an unwilling outsider trapped for the purpose. For them, in the words of Oroge, "No one in his senses would do such a job" (p. 254). Such, then, is the burden—its weight but not its detail is defined—which Eman assumes on behalf of strangers. The martyr is often a man who in the eyes of the world is out of his mind. His conduct is inexplicable in terms of a selfish rat race in which each man fends for himself. But as Soyinka reiterates in his work, without this type of self-sacrificing man society cannot be saved (even temporarily) from itself.

Eman's path is essentially a lonely one from the start. The main value for him of the traditional period of initiation is the opportunity it gives for individual labor and solitary contemplation. As for the specific ritual, "It is a small thing one can do in the big towns" (p. 269). He points out the significance of the period for him to Omae in one of the flashbacks to his earlier life:

This is an important period of my life. Look, these huts, we built them with our own hands. Every boy builds his own. We learn things, do you understand? And we spend much time just thinking. At least I do, it is the first time I have had nothing to do except think. Don't you see, I am becoming a man. For the first time, I understand that I have a life to fulfil.

And a little later, "A man must go on his own, go where no one can help him, and test his strength" (p. 266). This is the lonely road of the man of genius, whose renewing influence society sorely needs.

When Eman discovers the hollowness of his tutor—the latter is one of Soyinka's many false prophets and leaders—he suddenly leaves the place of initiation, having got all he wants out of it, and goes on a lonely pilgrimage. Once he has made up his mind, nothing can stop him. Omae's pathetic attempts to hold him

back—he actually drags her along as she clings to him—are
paralleled by the fruitlessness of Sunma's attempts to make him
leave her village and its evil. All the essential decisions for
Eman are personal ones made after a lonely internal struggle. In
this lies the uniqueness of this type of character; from it also
arises his seeming callousness to the normal human ties—of love,
for example. The pilgrim (another favorite figure for the type—
see "Idanre" for another example) has to leave all and follow
his chosen life: "Nothing ties me down" (p. 269).

Eman's sacrifice really ends the play. The possible effects on
society are only faintly suggested. His effect on Sunma is clear;
she will never be the same again after having met and worked
with him, but she is an ordinary individual, without Eman's
strength. (His death and her very isolation might possibly produce the necessary strength.) Oroge's momentary glimpse of
something in Eman's face at the height of the chase has been
noticed earlier. (Will anything come of it?) The most general
effect is seen in the horrified reaction of the villagers at the sight
of him hanging on the tree. In the words of Jaguna himself, who
is totally unmoved by the sacrifice, "One and all they looked up
at the man and words died in their throats" (p. 275). They should
have poured their curses on the helpless victim, but the sight of
their selfless benefactor hanging dead penetrated to a sensitive
vein. They "fled" their leaders. That is all the reaction. How far
will this experience take them? How effectively will the already
threatened reprisals of Jaguna kill the incipient reaction? We do
not know. It is apparently enough that the sacrifice has been
made and noticed. The silent set tableau on which the lights
fade at the end of the play represents a society still in need of
salvation.

[*Sunma, her last bit of will gone, crumbles against the wall. Some
distance away from them, partly hidden, stands the Girl, impassively
watching. Ifada hugs the effigy to him, stands above Sunma. The
Girl remains where she is, observing.*] (p. 275)

What price salvation?

Soyinka's use of scrambled chronology—a feature of *The
Interpreters*—is noteworthy here. The flashback which gives us
a glimpse of the past as a fill-in on the present is a favorite device
of the playwright. Faintly suggested in *The Swamp Dwellers*
(Makuri's narration of their wedding night's escapade in the

marsh), the technique is more elaborately exploited in *The Lion and the Jewel*. In *The Strong Breed* we have the backward flashes into Eman's past, some of which he watches from his position in the present of the play, thus giving an uncanny feeling of a suspension of the dimension of time. This effect is further heightened in the pageant at the end as Eman disappears from the play to his death behind the scenes, symbolically following the path of his father in what must be taken as his mental evocation of his father's last journey as carrier. Soyinka externalizes Eman's thoughts as he must have remembered his earlier attempts to renounce his inherited role, and the words of his father: "Your own blood will betray you son, because you cannot hold it back. If you make it do less than this, it will rush to your head and burst it open" (p. 261). He has now offered himself as a victim—a role he had declared himself unfitted for—but his body has flinched, and he is now running away from the ordeal. The sight of his father (in his mind, for the father had been long dead) revives his will, and he accepts his role, namely to follow in his father's footsteps (the metaphor is made flesh). "Wait father. I am coming with you … wait … wait for me father" (p. 274). It is the father's turn to flinch and to try in his paternal concern to divert his son from the path of martyrdom by pointing in the opposite direction. But Eman, with the words just quoted, follows his father to the symbolic river and to the real trap: *"There is a sound of twigs breaking, of a sudden trembling in the branches. Then silence"* (p. 274). Eman has made the supreme sacrifice.

Soyinka has used a fairly common scapegoat ritual as the vehicle for a tremendous moral statement which once again transcends its setting. One of the playwright's greatest strengths is his ability to manipulate symbols. This is as true of his plays as of his poetry. *The Strong Breed* succeeds in a way that another highly symbolic short radio play, *Camwood on the Leaves*,[7] does not. In the radio play both the symbols and what they represent retain their separate entities and operate independently. In *The Strong Breed* there is a complete fusion of object and symbol and a resulting greater suggestiveness.

V   The Trials of Brother Jero

The Trials of Brother Jero is a lighthearted satirical comedy based on the activities of the phony beach prophet, Brother

Jeroboam. The satire is there, but it is almost concealed by the predominating humor, which depends on a series of undiscovered identities which threaten at any moment to become known and upset the beach prophet's house of cards. As this rickety structure is rocked by one threat after another, the comedy of the play is generated.

Brother Jero is a self-confessed rogue who trades on the insecurities of his flock (his "customers" as he calls them in a moment of candor: "I know they are dissatisfied because I keep them dissatisfied. Once they are full, they won't come again." The audience is under no misapprehension about Brother Jero, who describes his approach to his "trade" from the very beginning of the play. Indeed, much of the comedy arises from the discrepancy between what the audience knows Brother Jero to be by his own confession and the front of holy hermit which he puts on for the benefit of his deluded gulls. The threat of his unmasking sustains the play, and once Chume discovers the true nature of his master, the whole structure threatens to collapse. Soyinka, however, saves the knave in order to make the play's final satirical point.

Chume is the classic victim of the prophet's method. The bane of his life is a wife whose constant scolding and nagging keep him on the edge of distraction. All the woman needs is, according to the desperate husband, "Just one sound beating. . . . But I've got to beat her, Prophet. You must save me from madness" (*Five Plays*, p. 213. Further citations in this chapter are in this volume.) Brother Jero knows this too, but the release which this beating would bring to Chume's frustrated spirit would deprive the prophet of his most faithful adherent. So he forbids Chume in the name of God to beat his wife. He confides in the audience: "If I do, he will become contented, and then that's another of my flock gone forever." The Prophet's grasp of human psychology is sound. But what he does not know is that the woman he is thus protecting is the same dreadful woman who has set up camp outside his house and threatens to keep up the siege until he settles his debt to her. In their double ignorance—Chume of the identity of Amope's debtor, Brother Jero of the relationship between Amope and Chume—lies a potential source of comedy which Soyinka exploits.

Amope's encounter with the unsuspecting prophet is pure comedy; it is the first threat to the prophet's carefully built-up image. He escapes from it only because the quarrelsome Amope, instead of maintaining her siege with single-mindedness, picks a side quarrel with a passing fishwoman during which Brother Jero gratefully escapes. The comedy of the encounter is both visual and verbal. Soyinka is a master of the funny physical situation, and one of his funniest is the discomfiture of the prophet as his careful preparations to climb out of his window and steal away unseen by Amope are shattered by her almost casual *"without looking round,"* question: "Where do you think you're going?" At which, according to the playwright's stage direction *"Brother Jero practically flings himself back into the house"* (p. 207). Brother Jero's obvious disadvantage in relation to the entrenched Amope makes him vulnerable so that his attempts to bluff Amope with the prophet façade soon crumble, and the holy man has to scale down his stance from the single-minded prophet insisting on his right to be left free to do the work of Christ, to the suppliant pleading to be permitted to get the money out of his savings bank account. Amope is practiced both in repartee and abusive complaint (as poor Chume knows), and she completely demolishes the prophet's façade first with cool repartee then with her indictment:

Jero: [*coughs*] Sister . . . my dear sister in Christ . . .
Amope: I hope you slept well, Brother Jero. . . .
Jero: Yes, thanks be to God. [*Hems and coughs*] I—er—I hope you have not come to stand in the way of Christ and his work.
Amope: If Christ doesn't stand in the way of me and my work.
Jero: Beware of pride, sister. That was a sinful way to talk.
Amope: Listen, you bearded debtor. You owe me one pound, eight and nine. You promised you would pay me three months ago but of course you have been too busy doing the work of God. Well, let me tell you that you are not going anywhere until you do a bit of my own work.
Jero: But the money is not in the house. I must get it from the post office before I can pay you.

Only Amope's own inability to pass up an opportunity for new quarrels gives the prophet an escape from this tight situation.

Brother Jeroboam's problems with "the daughters of Eve" are not yet over. He suffers agonies of self-control as the young girl returning from her daily bath in the sea tantalizes the prophet with her body. When a little later a woman trader

runs past chasing the drummer boy, her skirt hitched up for the
chase exposing her limbs, the prophet cannot resist this second
feminine temptation, and gives chase. From this encounter he
returns *"a much altered man, his clothes torn and his face
bleeding"* (p. 220). The alternation between the devout prophet
lashing his flock into holy paroxysms and the woman chaser—
getting for once what he deserves—is good comedy. It is also
part of the exposure of the true nature of Jero, but so far only
to the audience.

Through all his adventures Brother Jero still just manages to
mask his unholy activities from his trusting flock, but it seems
to be only a matter of time before events catch up with him.
The first discovery, however, is his when, taking the opportunity
of the prophet's revelation of his own suffering at the hands of
"the Daughters of Discord," Chume pours out once again his
sufferings at the hands of his wife and incidentally reveals her
identity to the prophet. Brother Jero is just running into one of
his routine injunctions against wife-beating when the penny
drops: "Brother Chume did you say that your wife went to make
camp this morning at the house of a ... of someone who owes
her money?" (p 221). Brother Jero is unable to resist this obvious
chance of vicarious revenge against Amope and promptly gives
Chume permission to beat her. This decision generates more
comedy and a further development of the plot, for it leads to
Chume's discovery of the connection between Amope and the
prophet.

The second encounter between Chume and his wife is in
dramatic and comic contrast to their first appearance at the beginning of the play. The comedy here derives from the fact that
in the intervening period Chume has become transformed by
the prophet's permission from a tame henpecked husband to a
dominating male. First Amope's refusal to recognize the change,
then her shock when Chume's unwonted rough handling of
her makes the change obvious, produce hilarious comedy.
The visual comedy of Chume bundling his wife bodily to the
accompaniment of her piercing screams is lively enough. The
comic action takes another dramatic turn as Chume, in the
midst of all this activity, makes his discovery. The moment of
realization is tantalizingly delayed as he tries to get the screaming
woman to answer his questions: "Did I hear you say Prophet
Jeroboam?" "Woman, did you say it was the Prophet who owed

you money? Is this his house? Does he live here? ... Is Brother Jeroboam ... ?" Despairing of any answer from the screaming woman Chume turns to a bystander, gets his answer, and revelation dawns: "So ... so ... so ... so ..."

All would now seem to be set for Chume's confrontation with his master, and a final unmasking, but Soyinka turns away from the obvious ending and makes an even more telling point. Brother Jero's true nature is no surprise to the audience. He confessed his roguery from the start. An unmasking would have given some physical comedy, but little else. Soyinka introduces a new character, an MP who appears just when the prophet needs some prop of influence. Through his help, the prophet can deal with his erstwhile apprentice who has now become troublesome:

I have already sent for the police. It is a pity about Chume. But he has given me a fright, and no prophet likes to be frightened. With the influence of that nincompoop I should succeed in getting him certified with ease. A year in the lunatic asylum would go him good anyway. (p. 233)

The grimness of Chume's fate must not be missed in the general atmosphere of the comedy of the MP's eventual gullibility. That Chume can be treated so unjustly is a telling comment on justice. The plum position which Brother Jero dreams up for the MP too has a significance that may be lost in the general comedy: it is "Minister of War":

I saw the mustering of men, gathered in the name of peace through strength. And at a desk, in a huge gilt room, foreign nations hung on your word, and on the door leading into your office, I read the words, Minister of War. (p. 230)

The point is not laid on with a trowel, but the passage, together with the comment on political influence and justice, gives the end of the play and its comic satire a more acid taste. Brother Jero ends the play a more sinister figure than he began. His roguery is now allied to power. He can easily eliminate ordinary mortals like Chume, and, contrary to his deserts (but in keeping with the ways of the perverse world), he survives his day of ordeals and lives to plague his deluded countrymen further. For Brother Jero is a false prophet. His people look pathetically to him for leadership and he replies with deceit. The situation is capable of wider and more sinister applications.

VI   The Road

There will probably always be some question as to the ultimate value of whatever it is the Professor finds at the end of his search for the Word in *The Road*. Whatever the estimate of that particular treasure, the play is without doubt a most exciting piece of theater. *The Road* defies narrow classification; its moods range from the near tragic to the hilariously comic; it contains biting satire as well as religious and mystical speculation; it combines a grim realism with near abstract symbolism. It offers producer and actors an opportunity to blend these different characteristics into a harmonious theatrical event.

For the actors there is a whole range of challenging roles. The combination of rogue, mystic, and pundit that is the Professor is an obvious starring role, while the versatile mimic Samson should stretch the resources of a comic actor. It is mainly through the mimicry of Samson that the play slips out of the present and extends its range with personalities and scenes from both the past as well as the contemporary outside the actual events of the play. He is the main vehicle for the satirical humor, though this role is not confined to him in a play that is never without humor for long in spite of its grim subject—death. The near hysterical, fast-talking, gun-pulling Nigerian stage cowboy and timber truck driver, Say Tokyo Kid, is a contrast to the slow moving, sleep-craving ex-mammy-wagon driver, Kotonu, who carries the psychological weight of his traumatic road accidents like an albatross around his neck. Each one of the other speaking parts—Salubi the frustrated driver with the smelly mouth, the venal hemp-smoking policeman, Particulars Joe, and the politician Chief-in-Town—is a distinctive character. Even Murano who, being dumb, has not a line to speak, is to suggest his mystery by his movements as he limps, always in the shadows with one foot in each world, ministering with palm wine to the needs of the Professor and his varied crew. The layabouts alternate as symbols of a purposeless existence and as musicians who provide most of the music that is so intrinsic to the play.

The music too is as varied as the moods and themes which it accompanies. It ranges from the Christian organ music of the neighboring church through the guitar band of the layabouts to the energetic throbbing drumming of the drivers' festival. Music is used throughout suggestively and symbolically.

The stage set, a single one for the whole play, is similarly comprehensive. The road-side shack is a perfect set for a play whose characters and themes spring from the hazardous road. The "AKSIDENT STORE" which occupies one side of it is itself a *bolekaja* (mammy wagon), which with its stock of personal and mechanical relics of numerous road crashes and deaths, is a grimly realistic reminder of the proximity of death to these users of the road. This theme of death on the road is further symbolized by the spider web with its ever-watchful spider; Murano prods the web several times during the play to call attention to this parallel to the road as a source of sudden death. (The spider itself is also used in a simile of reproof for Kotonu's lethargy.) Death is further suggested by the grave-yard which can be seen through the shack, but the graveyard is also a link with the psychic motif which is also part of the play.

The Professor's obsessive search for "the Word" is the principal intellectual feature of the play. This search has taken him from the church, which has now disowned him, to the drivers' shack which in his more orthodox days he had persecuted. Through the open windows of the shack and the church we have a view of one version of the Word—"a bronze eagle on whose outstretched wings rests a huge tome." Soyinka's set thus offers a permanent group of pictorial reminders of the varying themes of the play.

Although the various worlds of the play are blended and interact with each other, it would be convenient to look at them separately. The broad background is the world of the users of the road—drivers, their touts, their passengers, and general hangers-on. Through the drivers and their festival, the psychic theme is introduced. These users of the road, as the words of the play underline, are constantly exposed to death: "The road and the spider lie gloating, then the fly buzzes along like a happy fool." (*The Road*, p. 34. Further citations in this chapter are to this volume.) In addition to this constant dicing with death, they interact with policemen, forgers of licenses, looters, and spare parts salesman. All of them are linked by the phenomenon of death, which is never absent from the scene for long. Kotonu dramatizes this precariousness of the drivers' existence and their rapid turnover by his rhetorical catalogue of departed heroes of the road:

> Where is Zorro who never returned from the North with-
> out a basket of guinea-fowl eggs? Where is Akanni the
> lizard? I have not seen any other tout who would stand on
> the lorry's roof and play the samba at sixty miles an hour.
> Where is Sigidi Ope? Where is Sapele Joe who took on
> six policemen at the crossing and knocked them all into
> the river?
>
> Samson: Overshot the pontoon, went down with his lorry. (p. 21)

Kotonu's chronicle links the excitement of the road with the fact
of death. The heroes have gained immortality and passed into
legend through death. As Kotonu recites the chronicle, there is
a combination of glory and tragedy. Soyinka enlarges the drivers'
world by giving them a mythology of their own, arising from the
road and linked with death on the road.

One of the triumphs of the play is its portrayal of the many-
faceted nature of death. Side by side with the tragedy and the
myth we have grim physical pictures of death at speed and
its consequences. This transformation is fascinating to the Professor, who describes the scene of an accident to Kotonu:
"Come then, I have a new wonder to show you...a madness
where a motor-car throws itself against a tree—Gbram! and
showers of crystal flying on broken souls" (pp. 10-11). The
Professor goes on to paint an even grimmer picture of the scene,
which emphasizes the quick onset of physical decay after death
in the tropics: "It is a market of stale meat, noisy with flies and
quarrelsome with old women" (p. 11). The two pictures, coming
so close to each other as they do, complement one another.
The souls may be airborne in a shower of crystal, but the
bodies rapidly decay. Soyinka portrays the messiness of death
and the incongruities it produces, in several passages. Say
Tokyo Kid recalls in his racy language the scene of an accident
that he had come upon:

> You know, just last week I pass an accident on the road. There was
> a dead dame and you know what her pretty head was spread with?
> Yam porrage. See what I mean? A swell dame is gonna die on the
> road just so the next Passenger kin smear her head in yam porrage.
> (pp. 27-28)

Once a crash has taken place it also becomes a source of
business. The Professor may talk about the psychic aspects of
death, but he has always been the brains behind the AKSIDENT

STORE. It was he who had invited Sergeant Burma now dead—his brakes failed going down a hill—to open the store, and he is disappointed at the "tardiness" of Kotonu (whom he has now appointed to succeed Sergeant Burma) in replenishing the stock by looting crashed vehicles. He reproves Kotonu and his friend Samson when they return empty-handed from the scene of an accident. His first speech to them conceals his real meaning under words like "revelation" and "broken words," but his second speech makes his meaning unmistakably clear. (The two speeches also bring out the ambiguity of the Professor's nature. How seriously are we to take his constant verbalizing about a mystical Word, revelations, and Quests, when they are immediately coupled with quests for spare parts?)

Prof.:   And you brought no revelation for me? You found no broken words where the bridge swallowed them?
Samson: How could we think of such a thing Professor?
Prof.:   A man must be alert in each event. But the store then? Surely you brought new spare parts for the store?
Samson: Sir. . . .
Prof.:   You neglect my needs and you neglect the Quest. Even total strangers have begun to notice. . . . They complained of your tardiness in re-opening the shop. (p. 55)

This is the business aspect of the road. It is not to be obstructed by the campassionate aspects of death. Sergeant Burma had been made of sterner stuff; sentiment never got in the way of business: "He told me himself how once he was stripping down a crash and found that the driver was an old comrade from the front. He took him to a mortuary but first he stopped to remove all the tyres" (p. 21).

Some men like Sergeant Burma (in his case, calloused by his war experiences in Burma) develop sufficient detachment to reconcile them to the phenomenon of death. Others like Kotonu cannot develop the necessary hardness and become psychological victims of the road. He is finished as a driver and, it appears, even as a manager for the AKSIDENT STORE.

The play portrays drivers and their touts as professionals, with a fierce pride in their own special types of vehicle and the special skills which their particular type of work demands. Indeed, Samson who takes pride in his title of Champion Tout of Motor Parks despises the layabouts for their lack of professional pride: "Look at all these touts still sleeping. They have no pride in their job. Part-time tout part-time burglar. In any case, they are the pestilence of the trade. No professional dignity" (p. 3). Say Tokyo Kid displays his professional pride as he describes the hazards of wrestling with the spirits of a guy of timber on the back of his truck: "You wanna sit down and feel that dead load trying to take the steering from your hand. You're kidding? There is a hundred spirits in every guy of timber trying to do you down cause you've trapped them in, see?" (p. 26). Samson re-creates Sergeant Burma similarly recounting his skill with large oil tankers. This professionalism is no different from that of a boxer or a surgeon; it is one of the sustaining elements in the drivers' hazardous world.

Apart from their constant duel with death on the roads, drivers have to contend with authority in the form of policemen represented here by Particulars Joe. They have learned to live with this kind of authority. The policeman has to be bribed and hoodwinked with forged documents. Soyinka's treatment of the authority of the law is mainly satirical. In the play's first play-within-a-play, Samson and Salubi parody the police force in a piece depicting institutionalized corruption. Salubi's parody of the Lord's Prayer—"Give us this day our daily bribe"—introduces a parody of order by which in strict order of seniority—"officers first"—the police parade in front of Samson the millionaire to receive their bribes. Samson's commendatory comment—"Now that is what I call a well disciplined force"—is a perfect representation through irony of the total inversion of values of a corrupt authority. Particulars Joe as he shares hemp with the political thugs and looks for bribes in unexpected places—"Money has been left for me in more unlikely places"—merely mirrors the corruption of his superiors. He helps to complete the real world of the drivers and the road, and he also functions as a vehicle for satire. The Professor too in his role of forger of licenses is another constituent of the drivers' world as well as being a vehicle of satire on a corrupt society.

With all the ingredients of the drivers' world as described, *The Road* is rich enough. Soyinka, however, uses this as a back cloth for the "part psychic, part intellectual grope of Professor towards the essence of death." It has been shown that death is an ever-present feature of the drivers' world: death as tragedy and death as business. The Professor's search is for something more, something which he calls "the Word"—the prefatory note explains it as "the essence of death."

The character of the Professor is an enigma. Soyinka probably wants it to remain so, and it is therefore probably vain to look for a psychological unity in him. Most people take him for a madman, and he certainly displays a disorientation with his surroundings which is one of the manifestations of madness. Of all Soyinka's characters he is most like those characters who float on the edges of sanity and society in the plays of Samuel Beckett and Harold Pinter (to name just two writers of the Absurd School), though Soyinka's Professor has a quality of vigor which is absent from the characters of those playwrights.

Although the Professor is now outside regular society, he is near enough to it. We are constantly reminded of the days when he had been part of regular society. He still spends most of his time literally under the shadow of the church, and his language constantly echoes the liturgy of the church which he has now had to leave. Even his clothes—"tails and top-hat etc."—we are told by Samson are the relics of his evensong outfit in those more conventional days. Through mime, Samson gives us a history of the Professor's relations with the church which the man himself supplements. The Professor's severance from the church had not been voluntary, and thus the implication in some of his speeches of a deliberate abandonment of a false trail to the Word, is to that extent suspect (like most other things about the Professor, one is forced to admit). This is the suggestion, for example, in his explanation to Kotonu of his break with the church. He explains how in those earlier days, and in his enthusiasm for what he thought was "the Word" he had waged a holy war on the side of the church against drinking shacks: "Oh the Word is a terrible fire and we burned them by the ear. Only that was not the Word you see, Oh no, it was not. . . . And I left the Word hanging in the coloured light of sainted windows" (pp. 68-69). This suggests a deliberateness which is contradicted by his later account of how he was thrown out for a highly unorthodox interpretation to his Sunday school pupils of the rainbow, "while there was the spirit of wine upon me" (p. 89). (A drunken Sunday school teacher is hardly likely to have a clear sight of the eternal verities.) There are also nagging reminders of his having pilfered the funds of the church: "It is, I think, likely that I left the church coffers much depleted

...but I remember little of this" (p. 69). Haughtily though the Professor dismisses his fraud, he is still worried by its possible legal consequences. All this (and in spite of his insistence on correct grammar and correct music) does not add up to any inspiring picture of the Professor as a devoted or clear-sighted seeker of "the Word" while he was a member of the church. His severance therefore does not have any claim either to heroism or to visionary clear-sightedness.

The Professor's previous credentials are thus highly dubious. His present search for "the Word" is similarly deprived of purity by the conflicting elements in his character. It is possible, because of the corrupt nature of the surrounding society, to forgive him for making part of his living by forging licenses and other official documents. The Professor, however, is a parasite on the users of the road, charging them exorbitantly for his services to the very limits of their resources. Not only that, but when their backs are turned he even dips into their money bags. Samson catches him red-handed doing just this, but once caught, he brazenly legitimizes his act:

[*Samson goes. As he turns his back, Professor tries to extract a coin from the bag but Samson looks back just then. Professor is left with no choice but to carry out his action after a natural hesitation, explaining quite calmly*]
          For initial expenses you know.

Samson's brave attempt to nail the Professor's act for what it is merely produces one of the master's feats of verbal legerdemain which has the desired effect of reducing poor Samson to confusion:

Samson: With all due respects Professor sir, I don't quite see how that will come under initial expenses.
Prof.:   We had to get rid of him. Or you can have him spying on us if you like.
Samson: But Professor, he was already outside.
Prof.:   That is why it was necessary to call him in.
[*Samson scratches his head, puzzles it a bit, gives up.*]   (p. 62)

The Professor's preoccupation with the business side of death has been referred to earlier. If Salubi is to be believed, he is not above causing the occasional accident himself to ginger up the flow of spare parts into the AKSIDENT STORE: "Tell him the day the police catch him I will come and testify against him. The man is a menace. Pulling up road-signs and talking all that mumbo-jumbo" (p. 32).

Soyinka quite deliberately gives the Professor these unprepossessing aspects to his character, and yet he gives him also the role of a seeker of "the Word," a role in which he fitfully achieves a measure of profundity. He certainly gives the impression of someone who has in his sights something that others cannot see. It is this search that brings in the mystical elements of the play and links the Christian religion with the *egungun* mask through the Professor's exploration of both.

In keeping with his elevated role of seeker of "the Word," Soyinka gives the Professor a very impressive speech register redolent with suggestions of the Bible and church liturgy. This register is potentially ironic, for it gives the Professor's speech an impressive ring which, however, when put beside other things —his clothes and his conflicting roles—is capable of bathos. There is such a process going on at his first appearance. He enters clutching a road sign with the word BEND on it, "*in a high state of excitement, muttering to himself*":

Almost a miracle . . . dawn provides the greatest miracles but this . . . in this the dawn has exceeded its promise. In the strangest of places . . . God God God but there is a mystery in everything. A new discovery every hour—I am used to that, but that I should be led to where this was hidden, sprouted in secret for heaven knows how long . . . for there was no doubt about it, this word was growing, it was growing from earth until I plucked it. . . . (p. 8)

There is certainly an impressive prophetical tone here; the words come tumbling out as if from a man possessed, but when this mystery is seen to be identified with a road sign, much of the profundity which the words by themselves suggest is taken away. This of course is not "the Word" with a capital "W," but nevertheless the Professor's words endow it with mystery and significance. (All the time too, as has been suggested, his extraordinary attire contributes to the process of deflation.)

There are occasions when bathos is not so obviously suggested, and the Professor's voice momentarily becomes less equivocal, but as this is never sustained, he seems constantly teetering between profundity and bathos. The mystic and the proprietor of the AKSIDENT STORE are never far from each other. If the

proximity of the two roles makes it difficult to accept him as a
true mystic—a single-minded seeker after something profound
and important—it also makes it difficult to dismiss him altogether
as a charlatan.

His compulsive search for "the Word" among useless bits of
paper is so unpromising as to be a symptom of madness. It is
tempting to see the Professor—in a play which makes so much use
of parody—as a parody of the academic and the learned professional. He is the living image of the absent-minded professor,
turning up in the wrong place and scrutinizing with the aid of
a magnifying glass pieces of paper which to the uninitiated would
appear as useless as the discarded football pools coupons over
which the Professor so intently pores. This parody there certainly
is, but in the very intensity of the search also lurks the suggestion
that there just might be something in these unlikely places—
out of the mouths of rogues and madmen, as it were.

The Professor's search is not confined to bits of paper and road
accidents, however. Murano has provided him with an unexpected key to the mystery if only he could use it. Murano has
been knocked down by Kotonu's lorry while in a state of
possession—in the state of "transition from the human to the
divine essence" (note "For the Producer")—and the Professor
happens upon him abandoned by Kotonu and Samson in the back
of the lorry. In this *agemo* phase, Murano has one foot in each
world; to symbolize this duality, Soyinka gives him a heavy limp:

When a man has one leg in each world, his legs are never the same.
The big toe of Murano's foot—the left one of course—rests on the
slumbering chrysalis of the Word. When that crust cracks my friends
—you and I, this is the moment we await. (p. 45)

In trying to make use of Murano in this way the Professor is
playing with fire; he is in fact trying to use a god, Ogun, for
his own purposes. He realizes the danger of this sort of thing
and warns Samson off trying to pierce the mystery of Murano's
identity: "Those who are not equipped for strange sights, fools
like you—go mad or blind when their curiosity is pursued. First
find the Word..." (p. 45). The Professor seems at first to be
content to "await" the moment, not to hasten it. In one sense,
his whole search is one of waiting patiently: "Like you I also
wait but you do not hear me complain" (p. 60). But it is a most
aggravating wait, with his hands so to speak actually on the

key (Murano). Finally he can wait no more, and, seeing an opportunity (in Murano's reaction to the mask), he seizes the chance to force the secret out. Both the agony of the wait—for himself as well as for Murano—are conveyed in the words which lead to his desperate decision to "cheat" in order to understand:

And waiting, waiting till his tongue be released [*desperately*] in patience and in confidence, for he is not like you others whose faces are equally blank but share no purpose with the Word. So, surely Murano, crawling out of the darkness from the last suck of the throat of death, and Murano with the spirit of the god in him, for it came to the same thing, that I held a god captive, that his hands held out the day's communion! And should I not hope, with him, to cheat, to anticipate the final confrontation, learning its nature baring its skulking face, why may I not understand. . . .
[*He stops, looks around him.*]
So, why don't you ask him you runaway driver, why don't you ask him to try it on, see if it fits. . . .
[*He pulls up Murano, takes him into the store, pulls the canvas behind him.*] (pp. 90-91)

The Professor's act here is an attempt to reconstruct the state of possession—to bring the god Ogun into the store, and in some way to find the answer to his riddle. Having lost his patience, he will "anticipate the final confrontation." This "confrontation" leads in a rather indirect way to his death. The Professor still hopes as he approaches the confrontation that his dangerous experiment will reveal the answer without exacting the ultimate price (this is an almost Faustian situation): "I must hope, even now. I cannot yet believe that death's revelation must be total, or not at all" (p. 93). The danger of the experiment is realized by all in the store. Salubi tries to sneak out, and the frightened band has to be forced to play by the Professor's now over-whelming authority: "Play you croakers play." Events have now been set in train for a climax which is to involve the deaths of Say Tokyo Kid and the Professor himself, but in rather unexpected ways.

Made desperate by fear, Say Tokyo Kid interrupts the course of events by smashing the gourd which the Professor is carrying. But instead of a contest between the Professor and Say Tokyo Kid it is the possessed *egungun*, whom Say Tokyo Kid engages. This is an act of sacrilege of which perhaps only the impulsive, trigger-happy Say Tokyo is capable, simply because he is incapable of anticipating the consequences. The Professor, on the other hand, goes into all this with his eyes open. The knife which Salubi slides onto Say Tokyo during this fight is thus not meant to be used on the Professor but on the *egungun* with whom Say Tokyo is struggling. But the Professor tries to intercept it and is stabbed by Say Tokyo. His death therefore is given the appearance of an accident and hence seems to lose direct connection with his experiment. Say Tokyo it is who feels the direct wrath of the god. He is humbled for his presumption. As he pulls the knife out of the Professor's back, presumably to attack the *egungun*, the latter *"appears to come to life suddenly, lifts Say Tokyo in a swift movement up above his head, the knife out and in Say Tokyo's hand, smashes him savagely on the bench. Say Tokyo tries to rise, rolls over into the ground and clutches the train of the mask to him"* (p. 96).

The Professor's death at the hands of Say Tokyo Kid—instead of at the hands of an outraged god—is unexpected, and seems to underline Soyinka's ambiguous portrayal of both the man and his quest. We are still left wondering about his search and how much there had been in it. Soyinka does not usually give his characters perorations at the moment of death, but the Professor dies with a Jacobean peroration on his lips, the import of which seems to be as ambiguous as everything else about him. It has the sounds of a "moral" without being one. It has the externals of a final revelation without revealing anything.

What, for instance, are we to make of the Professor's parting advice to his survivors in the shack to "power your hands with the knowledge of death"? How is this to be done? The series of images which follows in expansion of this injunction suggest that it means that somehow the Professor's hearers should develop the gift of anticipating the fact of death—of seeing it before it comes. "In the heat of the afternoon when the sheen raises false forests and a watered haven, let the event first unravel before your eyes." Mirages, a frequent cause of accidents for hot and tired drivers, have been referred to before in the play. Professor too encountered mirages in his search for "the Word." He had called his curious mistake at the beginning of the play a "mirage" and had counseled his followers to "Avoid mirages—I had one this morning" (p. 35). This final injunction suggests, too, that the users of the road should be able to see past the mirage to the resulting accident and death—they are apparently unable to prevent it, however. What is the use of such a knack even if it can be developed—this ability to see your own death just before it comes—a quick opportunity for stocktaking or repentance? The Professor never talks about this. The other images which represent this ability to see death before it comes reinforce the first but still do not reveal any profound secret.

The injunction "to breathe like the road. Be the road" is expanded as an injunction to develop the treachery of the road. The image of the unsuspected snake is a parallel one to the spider/fly image used earlier in the play: "Coil yourself in dreams, lay flat in treachery and deceit and at the moment of a trusting step, rear your head and strike the traveller in his confidence. Swallow him whole or break him on the earth." Here the Professor does little more than reiterate the treacherous qualities of the road. Why are they to develop this treachery themselves?

I do not believe that the playwright expects anyone to derive eternal wisdom from the Professor. If he has at last found "the Word," he has found it for himself, and he does not communicate it. He is of no more use to his hearers than the dumb Murano. Viewed like this, the suggestion is that each one must find the essence of death for himself—in death. The long trail of the Professor has led everyone else nowhere. He has left the enigma behind him. There is an even more sardonic interpretation of the end of the play. What, if after all, there is no Word?[8] The play like its main character remains an enigma.

Through all the meanderings in search of the elusive Word, Soyinka's skill as a playwright remains constant. *The Road* contains a running satirical commentary on chosen aspects of life which sustains the play, whatever we make of the nature of "the Word." An exhaustive list of the butts of the play's satire is not necessary. It encompasses the whole of its society, and the picture which emerges of that society is not a flattering one. Through Chief-in-Town and his recruitment of thugs as his bodyguard for political meetings, we have a thrust at the violent political methods which brought disaster and an end to civilian politics in Nigeria for a while. The brief portrait is an ominous warning through comedy of the breakdown of order. Particulars Joe, the representative of the law, because of his total lack of integrity becomes himself a threat to order. Faith in the system he represents is shown to be crumbling in the drivers who find it less trouble and expense to buy forged licenses than to subject themselves to driving tests. The results of this self-licensing process on road safety are all too clear in the incidence of death on the roads. The cycle of corruption and the products of corruption reinforcing corruption is a never-ending one.

Organized religion comes in for its share of the satire. The picture of the church that emerges as we see it through Salubi's mimicry is a combination of vanity—in the sense of a preoccupation with externals—and corruption. Salubi's comment is an apt condemnation: "Dat one no to church, na high society" (p. 15).

In a situation like this there seems to be no hope from the top of society which is manned by false leaders, preoccupied only with their own vanity and well-being. Again it is through Samson (as millionaire) that we have a satirical glimpse at the methods of self-refreshment and renewal used by the rich and powerful of the society:

Now I want you to take the car—the long one—and drive along the Marina at two o'clock. All the fine fine girls just coming from offices, the young and tender faces fresh from school— give them lift to my house. Old bones like me must put fresh tonic in his blood.

It is Samson too who gives us the quick glimpse of the rags-to-riches story of the messenger who became a senator via a football pools win: "A friend of mine—he was a messenger—sent in one of these. He won thirteen thousand. Now he owns half the houses in Apapa and they have made him a Senator. You never know, you see" (p. 66).

There is a quick sideswipe at one of the absurd aspects of war—a topic more fully treated in "Idanre" and A Dance of the Forests—in Particulars Joe's reminiscence of his and Sergeant Burma's part in the world war when they enjoyed the luxury of killing people who had never done them any harm. His reflection is loaded with unconscious irony: "It is peaceful to fight a war which one does not understand, to kill human beings who never seduced your wife or poisoned your water" (pp. 81-82). Soyinka's neat reduction of war to this level of absurdity is of the same order as the urbane comment of the Court Historian commenting on Mata Kharibu's war in A Dance of the Forests; he is similarly oblivious of the ironic implications of his comment: "I mean this is war as it should be fought ... over nothing ... do you not agree?" (*Five Plays*, p. 62).

Through its satirical thrusts, the play extends its moral range over a wide area far beyond the immediate world of the road. Over the doings of men hover the higher beings whose presences men recognize, with whom they seek contact in life, and to whom they are reunited in death. The christian God through the church, Ogun through Murano and the drivers' festival, the spirits of timber, as well as the spirits of the graveyard constitute a veritable cloud of witnesses against whose more absolute standards the deeds of men are measured. With them the universe of the play is complete, embracing all from the dogs slaughtered on the road as "Ogun's meat" to the unseen presences themselves. *The Road* treats an essentially tragic theme without solemnity; it looks death in the face without losing its humor; it is an extraordinary theatrical achievement.

VII Kongi's Harvest

Like much of Soyinka's work, *Kongi's Harvest* is a great deal more subtle than it appears on the surface. It is a perfectly satisfactory play, even if it is taken only as the representation of a clash between a modern dictatorship and the traditional system which it has effectively replaced. It is that, but it is also a great deal more; it is ultimately a representation of the clash between life-giving forces and death-producing forces. The language of the play constantly links some characters with life and growth, others with death in a way which makes the presentation to Kongi of the head of Segi's father a fitting symbolic climax of this more fundamental struggle.

"Hemlock," the opening section, is a thematic microcosm of the whole play. Indeed, much of what a thematic analysis of the the play eventually yields is summarized in the three images which open the satirical anthem with which it begins:

> The pot that will eat fat
> Its bottom must be scorched
> The squirrel that will long crack nuts
> Its footpad must be sore
> The sweetest wine has flowed down
> The tapper's shattered shins.[9]
> (*Kongi's Harvest*, p. 1. Further citations
> in this chapter are to this volume.)

The first two images (they are Yoruba proverbs) contain the idea that every desirable end exacts its price. This applies not only to Kongi's "self imposed herculean assignment" as Oyin Ogunba suggests[10] but also to the equally herculean task of trying to unseat him, a task which ends in disaster, thus exacting its price without the satisfaction of achieving the end. This last idea is reiterated in the third image. In mockery of the tapper's efforts—"his shattered shins"—the sweetest wine has flowed uselessly away.

Even the satirical opening of the play has obliquely (so obliquely that its real significance is realized only through hind-sight) presented in imagery a situation of fruitless labor. The jingling anthem goes on further to portray the prevailing political situation. The new regime built on new political theories—the isms of Ismaland—has contemptuously displaced the old:

> To demonstrate the tree of life
> Is sprung from broken peat
> And we the rotted bark, spurned
> When the tree swells its pot
> The mucus that is snorted out
> When Kongi's new race blows.   (p. 1)

The anthem is satirical and ironic. The old regime portrays itself in the words which the "new race" would use. (Oba Danlola repeats this style of ironical self-mockery frequently in the play.)

The new regime depends for its continuance on its own propaganda; the "government loud speaker" is thus central to their political machinery. In Ismaland this is a device which pours out propaganda but admits of no reply—even if reply were worthwhile: "My ears are sore/ But my mouth is *agbayun*" (p. 2). This tyranny of words is later given physical shape in the Reformed Aweri Fraternity (a parody of its traditional prede-cessor) which, in its isolated word factory, manufactures the words which go into the talking boxes. The satirical anthem silently comments on the value of such words—the very repetition of "words" throughout the anthem effectively devalues their worth. When the Reformed Aweri actually appear and are seen in conclave, literally producing the words to order, the deval-uation of the coinage becomes complete.

The Superintendent is the first manifestation of the new race in the play. Invested with the insignia of the new era—"Khaki and brass buttons"—he tyrannizes over the Oba who is now in his power. His action of silencing the royal drums is symbolic of his power conferred on him by the new regime. But his power over the Oba is only physical. This is inconvenient enough (for the Oba), but it is shown to be essentially limited. The Oba has spiritual resources which Kongi does not have and therefore cannot pass on down to the functionaries of his regime. All the Superintendent's bluster is knocked out of him when the Oba threatens to prostrate before him. The Superintendent is not so remote from his origins as to risk the implied curse of this gesture and is soon reduced to self-abasement and abject pleading before the physically powerless Oba:

I call you all to witness. Kabiyesi, I am only the fowl droppings that stuck to your slippers when you strutted in the back yard. The child is nothing, it is only the glory of his forbears that the world sees and tolerates in him. (p. 6)

The father/child relationship which the Superintendent here acknowledges is the elusive relationship which Kongi does not have with his subjects. His authority is not similarly rooted in tradition and in the minds of the governed. (The play suggests that his authority is detached from nature too. It has no anchor.) It is this lack of a deep-seated base which accounts for the insecurity and lack of poise, as well as for the brutality of Kongi's regime. The ambiguity of the Superintendent's plight—he tyrannizes over the Oba but ultimately fears him—mirrors the ambiguity of the whole of Kongi's regime. Even in prison, the Oba is still powerful: "Ogun is still a god/ Even without his navel." It is in the hope of capturing the Oba's spiritual authority that Kongi demands a public surrender of his authority by making the Oba ceremonially present the new yam to him in public.

The "Hemlock" section suggests also that a heavy responsibility accompanies the Oba's exalted position in the minds of his people. People (like Kongi) who envy this position and covet it do not realize the depth of this responsibility. The Oba is a protector of his people to the extent of being prepared to give his life in protection of their own. In the words of Sarumi, a junior Oba:

> They complained because
> The first of the new yams

> Melted first in an Oba's mouth
> But the dead will witness
> We drew the poison from the root. (p. 7)

Drawing the poison from the root, to make eating and living safe for the governed, is the ultimate responsibility of rule and its *raison d'être*. Without this kind of attitude to the ruled, the ruler is not entitled to their deep loyalty and reverence. This idea is fundamental to *Kongi's Harvest*. It is because the Oba's regime is based on this basic assumption that his regime emerges as being morally superior to the physically more successful regime of Kongi, which is based entirely on a shallow personality cult and a vicious selfishness. Kongi stands condemned because his is a regime that is self-centered, not people-centered. Ultimately it is a regime based on death, not on life. Far from drawing out the poison to give life to the people, Kongi is a dealer out of death.

The Oba is given even deeper spiritual links; his authority crosses the borders of life. He not only gives life to the already born but is linked with the bringing of new life into the world. His links with the unborn are suggested in Sarumi's words:

> Oh yes, we know they say
> We wore out looms
> With weaving robes for kings
> But I ask, is *popoki*[11]
> The stuff to let down
> To unformed fingers clutching up
> At life   (p. 8)

Seen in this light, the play is rescued from the facile opposition of old versus new. It is an opposition between the humane and the monstrous, between the giver of life and the bringer of death.

Even in this early section of the play, "Hemlock" portrays Kongi as a monster which should have been scotched before it achieved its full proportions. One parable makes the point:

Ogbo Aweri: Observe, when the monster child
              Was born, Opele taught us to
              Abandon him beneath the buttress tree
              But the mother said, oh no,
              A child is still a child
              The mother in us said, a child
              Is still the handiwork of Olukori.

Sarumi: Soon the head swelled
                    Too big for pillow
                    And it swelled too big for mother's back
                    And soon the mother's head
                    Was nowhere to be seen
                    And the child's slight belly
                    Was strangely distended. (p. 10)

The monster child Kongi to whom this parable is applicable has become by slow degrees and, ironically through the merciful indulgence of his motherland, the smotherer, the destroyer of his country.

"Hemlock" thus sets the scene thematically for the main conflicts of the play and gives no false hope of a comfortable outcome. Even the title, "Hemlock," with its implication of poison and the death of Socrates,[12] indicates tragedy. Only disaster is predicted by the Oba as he dances his slow dignified dance:

                    Delve with the left foot
                    For ill-luck; once more
                    With the left foot alone, for disaster
                    Is the only certainty we know.[13] (p. 10)

The thematic microcosm of "Hemlock" is played out in the two main parts of the play, called simply "First Part" and "Second Part." Soyinka's stage directions require the two sets for the "First Part" to be on stage simultaneously, either being highlighted as it is required. Between these two sets representing "Kongi's retreat in the mountains" and Segi's nightclub, the Organising Secretary flits to and fro. The two areas of the stage represent opposing forces. Kongi's retreat is gradually revealed as a barren place of forced deprivation. Kongi himself is fasting— a fast which turns out, like his publicized desire for seclusion, to be a mere publicity stunt—for while pretending to be unaware of his presence, he strikes a number of poses for the benefit of an international press photographer. Kongi's asceticism is clearly exposed as a mere front. The Reformed Aweri too are kept virtually imprisoned with Kongi on a near starvation diet—the fifth Aweri continually complains that he is starving—dreaming up an "image" for themselves and for Kongi, and also manufacturing the words to go with their pasteboard façade. The total effect of the scenes in the retreat is one of barrenness, of a denial of life and truth, and all this, ironically, in preparation for a harvest.

Segi's nightclub is by contrast a scene of life. While the Kongi retreat is dimly lit, Segi's nightclub is lit with colored lights. There is music, dancing, and beer. Segi herself, a complex character, but unmistakable for her utter femininity, is an embodiment of the life principle. Daodu too is similarly suggestive of life. He works the land and hence is close to the source of life. The contrast between the two juxtaposed areas is total. When the Organising Secretary moves between the two, he is spanning a gap in a way which only a cold cynical professional like himself can do; he is negotiating between the forces of life and forces of death. He can partake of life—he drinks beer at Segi's club—but his profession does not allow him to let up and admit the fullness of life: "You know, I am very fond of music. Unfortunately I haven't much time for it. Moreover one would hardly wish to be found in this sort of place." The fundamental nature of the opposition of the two localities becomes clearer as the "First Part" develops.

The "First Part" opens with the Reformed Aweri in conclave; in the vocabulary of the new regime they are at a "planning session"—to solve "the problem of an image for ourselves." The Reformed Aweri are something of a parody of their predecessors, the traditional Aweri, whom they had displaced. The new men are insecure; their very concern for an image is indicative of their insecurity. They lack the style of their predecessors, as the First Aweri confesses, and are in obvious disarray. The Fifth Aweri demonstrates his weariness with the whole proceeding by ostentatiously going to sleep at intervals. Awake, the Aweri fare little better. Their confusion manifests itself in self-contradictory phrases like "youthful elders" and "modern patriarchs." They are men who have abandoned what they contemptuously call "proverbs and senile pronouncements" but do not yet understand the pseudoscientific jargon—"ideograms and algebraic quantums" —of Kongi's new political philosophy, "Scientificism."

The contrast between the Reformed Aweri and the Oba's court—even the rump of it that is left—is reminiscent of the contrast between the assurance of the Bale of Ilujinle in *The Lion and the Jewel* and the confused verbalizing of the school teacher Lakunle. Except when he is playacting, throwing dust in the eyes of the Organising Secretary in the "Second Part"— when he adopts a theatrically abusive style—the Oba's speech is dignified, weighted down with proverbs.

The Party Secretary is the focus of the two opposing forces. His job is to persuade the Oba, Daodu's uncle— "a damned stubborn goat, an obstructive, cantankerous creature and a bloody pain in my neck"—to surrender his power publicly to Kongi and thus (presumably) dethrone himself in the hearts of the people. Kongi hopes that this act will transfer the Oba's spiritual authority to him. It should be recognized that Kongi in his monstrous self-delusion has even greater ambitions than merely displacing the Oba. He wants to replace "the Spirit of Harvest," the presiding deity himself. As the Secretary explains to the Aweri: "Kongi desires that the king perform all his customary spiritual functions, only this time, that he performs them to him, our Leader. Kongi must preside as the Spirit of Harvest, in pursuance of the Five-Year-Development Plan" (p. 20). Kongi himself declares with manic insistence, emphasizing in successive repetitions "am," "Spirit," and "HAR-VEST," "I am the Spirit of Harvest" (p. 36-37).

That a man whose total personality amounted to a denial of life should so insistently seek to fill the position of giver of life is a measure of Kongi's self-delusion, but more importantly, it is a dramatization of the tragedy which such a reversal of fundamental values brings. Kongi's regime is a regime of repression. The Reformed Aweri are the instruments of intellectual and spiritual repression, while the mallet-swinging carpenters (their Captain is also superintendent of the Detention Camp) are the instruments of physical repression. As Kongi euphemistically puts it: "They [the Carpenters Brigade] complement my sleepy Aweris here. These ones look after my intellectual needs, the Brigade takes care of the occasional physical requirements" (p. 36).

That all Kongi's machinery of suppression goes little deeper than the flesh is shown by the occasional bomb-throwing which rocks his regime. This is the only kind of harvest over which Kongi is qualified to preside—a harvest of death. The bomb throwers of course have to be hanged, while the Reformed Aweri, on Kongi's orders, have to counter the effects of the bomb-throwing by organizing slogans around the key word "Harmony." It seems unlikely that even Kongi really places much faith in the effects of such words. Regimes like his are doomed to go on multiplying villainies. The Reformed Aweri, no less than the lower orders of the society, are pathetic victims of a regime of death. Their reaction, as the Organising Secretary announces the sentence on the bomb throwers, dramatizes their plight. The word "hanged" in the passage stuns even these hardened cynics into silence, but only momentarily until one of them can translate the brutality of "hanged" into the meaningless jargon of the new politics—"An exercise in scientific exorcism." Thus translated, the horror is covered with a façade of words, and they can approve the action. The section with the stage directions reads:

Secretary: And the key-word, Kongi insists, must be—Harmony. We need that to counter the effect of the recent bomb-throwing. Which is one of the reasons why the culprits of that outrage will be hanged tomorrow.
[*A nervous silence. They look at one another, stare at their feet.*]
Fourth: An exercise in scientific exorcism—I approve.
[*Followed by murmurs and head-nodding of agreement by the majority.*]

Thus men in a trapped situation, to keep their sanity—at least for a time—play tricks with words and lives. It is most effective that in the playwright's arrangement this scene of mute con-donation of death should be broken by loud chords on "guitar" which announce the shift to Segi's nightclub on the other side of the stage to which the Organising Secretary now ferries himself.

Segi's nightclub has been characterized as a contrasting scene of light and life to Kongi's retreat. It, and its habitués, deserve a closer look. In a general way, the nightclub represents the rest of the society. When the Organising Secretary comes into it for the first time, accompanied by "The Right and Left Ears of State," the reactions which the playwright requires are variously representative of differing characters and political persuasions. They are not all of one kind: "*A few night-lifers pick up their drinks and go in, there are one or two agressive departures, some stay on defiantly, others obsequiously try to attract attention and say a humble greeting*" (pp. 13-14). They represent the various reactions to a repressive regime: cowardly (frightened) retreat, surly disavowal, aggressive confrontation, obsequious coattailing. Presumably the faint hearts never come back, and the club becomes something of a center of opposition to Kongi's regime. The Left and Right Ears are in fact soon whisked away as political hostages.

Segi and Daodu are the focal points of this opposition to

Kongi's regime. Segi is another of Soyinka's extraordinary women
(Madame Tortoise and Rola in *A Dance of the Forests* and Simi
in *The Interpreters* are other manifestations). Her attraction for
men is certain and total. Even the Organising Secretary is not
unaffected. He is half fascinated, half frightened by her:

Does that woman have to keep looking at me like that?

      ❀   ❀   ❀

I just wish she'd ... what do they sing about her?
What are they saying?

Segi is an embodiment of sex and hence potentially at least of the
creative principle. However, hers is no easy relationship. She
turns men mad. Those who dislike and distrust her call her
dangerous and worse. The Organising Secretary calls her "witch";
Oba Danlola, "A right cannibal of the female species" (p. 51).
(It is interesting that the Oba subsequently recognizes her,
although grudgingly, as an ally.) Segi is heady wine as her
praise singers declare:

> The being of Segi
> Swirls the night
> In potions round my head
>
> But my complaints
> Will pass
>
> It is only
> A madman ranting
>
> When the lady
> Turns her eyes,
>
> Fathomless on those
> I summoned as my go-between. (p. 15)

Once tasted the effect is permanent:

> But Segi
> You are the stubborn strand
> Of meat, lodged
> Between my teeth
> I picked and picked
> I found it was a silken thread
> Wound deep down my throat
> And makes me sing.

Her inscrutability totally discomposes the Organising Secretary.
This inscrutability indeed pervades the whole club, making it
a milieu in which the cool Secretary cannot concentrate: "This
place bothers me" (p. 31). Apart from their brief encounter when
he first comes to the club, the lady herself speaks only once to
the Secretary, on the last of his visits to the club; he had shied
away from earlier contact when Daodu suggested it, and even
here the encounter is a frightening and fatiguing one for him:
"*Secretary stares at her, experiencing fear....*"(p. 42), and ('at
the end of a very brief exchange) "*sits down, dog-tired.*" Elaborate care is taken to build Segi up as a creature with hidden
depths and great resources. She has been a lover of Kongi; not
just a lover but one who had once believed in him and his
cause, and had been prepared to devote her resources to his
work: "Kongi *was* a great man, and I loved him" (p. 43). The
tense is significant. Now she is a woman who has lost her
faith: "If I could again believe ..." (p. 44). Her faith is now to
be put on Daodu. In spite of her poise and her apparent imper-
turbability, Segi is human and has feelings. She is a daughter
(whose father is in detention and is later killed), and she
knows moments of fear. She seems to be an element which all
human institutions need—devotion to life. She has abjured
the cause of death symbolized by Kongi and now clings to a
new hope in Daodu.

Daodu too is a complex character. He is a prince, being son
to the junior Oba Sarumi, and heir to Danlola's throne—a
throne which Kongi's regime makes little more than an empty
chair, except for its hidden spiritual resources. Daodu is thus
linked with the spirit of the people. He is also linked to the
earth, being a successful farmer. But he has also partaken of
the influences out of which the new regime of Kongi derives
its being. He has been abroad: "Lately returned from everywhere and still/ Trying to find his feet" (p. 54). He may be
still trying to find his feet, but he has not broken his traditional
links. After his wide experiences, he has gone back to the
earth and to his traditional role. In this lies his potential
strength. He has retained the links with humanity and with
the source of life, while opening himself to other influences.

One of the characteristics of Kongi is his asexuality. It is
another symbol of his denial of life. Daodu by contrast is shown
in a sexual role. Segi, who is the symbol of sex and hence of

reproduction and growth, invites Daodu to an almost symbolic acceptance of his sexual role on the eve of the harvest which is also to be the occasion for the challenge to Kongi's regime. Daodu at first resists this role, pleading business in preparation for the morrow. The exchanges are couched in growth and harvest symbols:

Segi: Come through the gates tonight. Now I want you in me,
           my Spirit of Harvest.
Daodu: Don't tempt me so hard. I am swollen like prize yam under
           earth, but all harvest must await its season.
Segi: There is no season for seeds bursting.
Daodu: My eyes of kernels, I have much preparation to make. . . .
Segi: I must rejoice, and you with me. I am opened tonight. I
           am soil from the final rains.   (p. 44)

Daodu eventually accepts the invitation, but not before a very significant choice of love and life is made at the insistence of Segi.

As Segi and her women drape the symbolic harvest robe about Daodu—he is to represent the Spirit of the Harvest—Segi, suddenly dramatizing the paramountcy of this role, kneels in front of him: "*She comes round, surveys him. Suddenly she kneels and clings to the hem of his robes.*[14] *The other women kneel too.*" Segi exclaims, "My prince . . . my prince," in a reverential tableau confronting Daodu with his role of opposition to Kongi. He pleads to be allowed to play it out through hatred, to match Kongi at his barren game. (Does this mean a straightforward armed revolution? or a regime which outmatches Kongi's in brutality?) But Segi urges him to play it out the other way through life and love:

Segi: My prince . . . my prince
Daodu: Let me preach hatred Segi. If I preached hatred I could
           match his barren marathon, hour for hour, torrent for
           torrent . . .
Segi: Preach life Daodu, only life . . .
Daodu: Imprecations then, curses on all inventors of agonies, on
           all Messiahs of pain and false burdens . . .
Segi: Only life is worth preaching my prince.
Daodu: [*with mounting passion*] On all who fashion chains, on
           farmers of terror, on builders of walls, on all who guard
           against the night but breed darkness by day, on all whose
           feet are heavy and yet stand upon the world. . . .
Segi: Life . . . life. . . .

Daodu: On all who see, not with the eyes of the dead, but with
           eyes of Death. . . .
Segi: Life then. It needs a sermon on life . . . love. . . .
Daodu: [*violent with anger*] Love? Love? You who gave love, how
           were you requited?
Segi: [*rises*] My eyes were open to what I did. Kongi *was* a
           great man, and I loved him.
Daodu: What will I say then? What can one say on life against
           the batteries and the microphones and the insistence of one
           indefatigable madman? What is there strong enough about
           just living and loving? What?
Segi: It will be enough that you erect a pulpit against him, even
           for one moment.
Daodu: [*resignedly*] I hate to be a mere antithesis to your Messiah
           of pain. (pp. 45-46)

For a moment Daodu is transformed by his symbolic robe. His
imprecations against the Kongis of this world are those of a
representative voice. He speaks for the forces of life against
the forces of death. To realize this, then, he cannot be another
Kongi, overthrowing his regime by instituting a bloodier one.
He has to overcome him by being what he in his resigned acceptance calls a mere antithesis, but an antithesis he must be.
This throws some light on the rather undramatic nature of the
morrow's gesture. It is to turn out to be just that, a gesture—
"a pulpit against him, even for one moment." The efficacy of
this type of gesture against the regime of "an indefatigable
madman" can almost be predicted. Here one is reminded of the
rallying cry which almost mocks itself, at the end of one of
Soyinka's own "Poems from Prison": "Orphans of the world/
Ignite!"[15] However resignedly, Daodu accepts his role and, in
symbolic celebration, the invitation of Segi. He thus unites with
his counterpart in the cycle of life and growth. He is ready for
his role of the morrow.

In contrast to this scene, the "First Part" ends with a quick
look at Kongi, the Messiah of pain, and he is seen in a fit of un-
controllable anger—it ends in an epileptic fit—as he decrees
death. Because one of his prisoners has escaped, he withdraws
his amnesty—it is only a word after all. His epileptic fit leaves
him struggling for breath and life, and hence a living symbol
of his regime of death.

The "First Part," then, has deployed the forces, with Daodu
taking the foreground as the protagonist of life. But his uncle

Oba Danlola is still Oba, and now that he has been released to present the new yam to Kongi, he resumes the foreground. Oba Danlola goes through an elaborate piece of playacting in order to deceive the Organising Secretary into thinking that he is preparing to make the formal presentation of the new yam to Kongi, an act he has no intention at this point of carrying out. Soyinka uses poetic registers subtly here. He gives the Oba his characteristic dignified imagic style when he is speaking his real thoughts, and a fruity, scatological, abusive style when he is playacting. His explanation of his deceptive preparations illustrates his two styles. In the first section of the passage he uses his natural style; in the second, he speaks in his newly adopted theatrical role of an enthusiastic supporter of Kongi, badly let down by his inept servants:

> When the dog hides a bone does he not
> Throw up sand? A little dust in the eye
> Of His Immortality will not deceive
> His clever Organising Secretary. We need to
> Bury him with shovelfuls.
> [*Re-enter Dende*]
>
> You horse-manure! Is this a trip
> To gather mangoes for the hawker's tray?
> Tell me, did I ask for a basket fit
> To support your father's goitre?   (pp. 48-49)

Even the Organising Secretary is taken in. That the Oba has to play this role is itself a sign of the times. The wily old man is playing the new regime's word game upon which the opening "anthem" had been such a telling comment, and he can be as good at the game as anyone else. He defends himself against Daodu's accusation (which would have been damning in other circumstances):

> You should, my son, when you deal in politics
> Pay sharp attention to the word. I agreed
> Only that I would prepare myself
> For the grand ceremony, not
> That I would go. Hence this bee hum fit
> For the world's ruling heads jammed
> In annual congress.

There is a seeming conflict in this section of the play between
the aims of the Oba and those of his heir. Daodu is seen in the
strange role of acting for the Organising Secretary in persuad-
ing his uncle to attend the festival and perform as Kongi wishes.
Indeed, the opposition between the two leads to a dramatic
climax when Daodu seizes the Oba's ceremonial whisk and
bursts the royal lead drum with it. This appears to be the final
act of disloyalty; even the Superintendent in "Hemlock" had
only seized the wrist of the drummer; he had not silenced the
drum finally:

> That prison
> Superintendent merely lay his hands
> On my lead drummer, and stopped
> The singing, but you our son and heir
> You've seen to the song itself. (p. 60)

Daodu's silencing of the song itself is a significant symbol of the
end of effective chieftaincy of the Oba's sort in the face of the
competition offered by modern political regimes. There is no
suggestion, however, that the particular manifestation of modern political power in Kongi's regime will survive either. Some
form of government which combines the moral authority and
humanity of the Oba's regime with the efficiency of modern
regimes (the Daodu/Segi combination) seems to be indicated
as the hope of stability. So although his personal loyalty to the
Oba is not really in dispute, Daodu's act performed "with sudden decision" is significant for the future of the society. It is an
open acknowledgment of the fact that a different road lies
ahead—a fact which the Oba's continued role playing had
tended to mask.

The Oba has now become part of Daodu's plan of the day—
"a vital part." It is significant that what finally persuades the
Oba to take part in the plan is the revelation to him of the true
identity of Segi against whom he had been so hostile:

Daodu: [*desperately*] The woman you warned me about, Segi, the
           witch of the night clubs as you labelled her, is the daughter
           of this man who has escaped. And she wants the Harvest
           to go as we all planned, as much as I.
           [*Danlola turns slowly round*]
Danlola: Is this the truth about that woman?
Daodu: The truth.

Danlola: [*hesitates and a far-seeing look comes into his eyes*] There
            was always something more, I knew, to that strange woman
            beyond her power to turn grown men to infants. (p. 63)

It is Segi, ironically, now recognized as an ally, whose participation reconciles the Oba to a plan the details of which he does
not even know.

All is now set for the climax (which in Soyinka's typical
style turns out to be a deliberate anticlimax). The preliminaries
to the arrival of Kongi confirm the earlier suggestions of the
nature of his regime. The music of penny whistles in contrast
to the royal drums demonstrates its shallowness for one thing.
Its repressive nature is symbolized by the heavy mallets of the
carpenters who will defend the "creed of Kongism" relentlessly:
"And heads too slow to learn it/ Will feel our mallets' weight."
That the regime's primary concern is with the surface of things
rather than with essentials is illustrated by the dreadful plight
of the speech-writing Aweri, who suddenly discovers that the
four-and-a-half-hour-long speech he had written for Kongi is
too short because the neighboring President has just spoken
for seven hours. The concern with triviality that this implies
is characteristic not only of the festival but of the whole of
Kongi's regime.

The entrance of Segi and her woman with their sarcastic songs
and defiant gestures helps to set the scene for a confrontation
which is to be signaled by Daodu's speech, especially when
Segi's women "form a ring around Daodu with their pestles"—at
which even the Organising Secretary retreats to a safe distance.
But the expected dramatic confrontation does not come.

Daodu's speech is wasted on Kongi who does not hear it,
and at the crucial point when the dethronement (possibly
assassination) of Kongi should have taken place, the sound of
gunfire heralds the death of Segi's father who, it transpires,
was to have done the crucial act. The plot obviously fails, and
Kongi goes on to make a triumphant speech as Daodu ruefully
comments: "There should have been no speech. We failed again"
(p. 81). The gift which throws Kongi off-balance in his moment
of triumph is a hastily thought up gesture by Segi to take the
place of the failed *coup*. In the middle of what is described as
"a real feast, a genuine Harvest orgy of food and drink" (p. 81),
Segi returns with a covered dish which is taken to be the fes-

tival yam, but *"In it, the head of an old man, Segi's father."*[16]
Thus, in the middle of the feast of life being celebrated by his
subjects, Kongi is given a harvest dish more symbolic of his
denial of life. This is a symbolic dramatization of the opposed
values of Kongi and his people—death against life. Kongi obviously takes the meaning of this symbolic curse on his regime—
"Kongi's mouth wide open in speechless terror" (p. 84). It is
not that he is afraid of the sight of physical death—by now he
must be inured to it—but he sees the eventual futility of his terror
staring back at him through the dead man's eyes.

Daodu's more dramatic revolution fails, and in this Soyinka
is consistent with his avoidance of grand dramatic endings in
which evil is put down and a brand-new regime of good succeeds. But the point has been made. Daodu (with the help of
Segi) has led an assertion of life against the death principle that
Kongi represents. Although it is unsuccessful, the mere assertion
keeps hope alive that this principle is still there, can reassert
itself, and in due course might prevail. For the time being
Kongi's barren "Scientificism" (the very clumsiness of the name
is satirical) prevails, but even in the midst of his barren cult,
his people can momentarily assert life in a *real* harvest feast.
Food, feasting, and sexual fulfillment in Soyinka's work are
usually symbolic of life. In his poem "Civilian and Soldier," the
civilian throws life in the face of the soldier in the form of
"meat and bread, a gourd of wine/ A bunch of breasts."

Daodu too represents the kind of force through which the
society can be saved. He has been shown to have the spiritual
sanctions necessary to establish continuity with the now out-
dated regime of Oba Danlola and carry over its spiritual authority
into the modern age—an age for which he is also equipped.
There is no certainty at the end of the play of the precise fate
of Daodu and Segi. The Oba himself seems to abandon flight
and "starts briskly back in the opposite direction," that is, back
into Ismaland, and since the symbolic "iron grating descends and
hits the ground with a loud, final clang," his end both as an
effective personal and traditional force can be said to have been
symbolically represented. The grating represents the general
"clamp-down" which the Organising Secretary predicts (p. 80)
and from which he flees. But whether Sarumi and his volun-
teers succeed in getting Daodu and Segi away is not clear. The
presumption is that they do not. The text suggests that Daodu

does not want to leave. Danlola describes the role of the party which has gone after him and Segi:

> If he's not already
> In Kongi's hands, they'll abduct him
> Forcibly and parcel him across the border.
> And that woman of his. (p. 89)

Daodu seems to be determined to stay and face the consequences of his action or continue his opposition within the country. The odds are against him whatever his intentions, but the odds are always loaded against the true savior of his society in Soyinka's work, who frequently has to make a sacrifice of himself in order to save the society. So whether Daodu falls into Kongi's hands and is killed or whether he is able to hold out in his farm settlement (hardly likely), his role would be fulfilled. He has released a spirit in the land. To the cynical Organising Secretary who cannot understand the meaning of sacrifice, Segi and Daodu are mad—"roadside lunatics." But they have definitely released a potential force which has infected even the old Oba, making him momentarily one in spirit with the revolution: "The strange thing is I think/ Myself I drank from the stream of madness/ For a little while."

There is an interesting parallel to Daodu's refusal to leave, with a situation in Soyinka's radio play *The Detainee*.[17] Konu, the detainee, is visited in prison by Zimole who has up to now protected Konu's children because of his position in the repressive regime. But even his position is now threatened, and he can no longer protect his friend's children. He can, however, send them out of the country where they will be safe from tyranny. But this offer Konu resolutely refuses: "If the worst happens, they should be here. Let them know what fear is, so they can choose to fight it or live with it. I want them all to have that choice. Don't take them out of the country, Zimole." This helps to explain the anticlimax with which *Kongi's Harvest* ends. The struggle merely continues; it is this continuity, however feeble, which holds out any hope for particular situations and societies and, eventually, for mankind.

VIII   Madmen and Specialists

Madmen and Specialists[18] was first produced in Waterford, Connecticut, in the summer of 1970, and it shows significant

developments in Soyinka's technique, developments which at
least by the benefit of hindsight could be seen as arising logically
from his earlier work.

For this play he has abandoned the traditional concern with
plot, and the portrayal of fixed characters. There is very little
story as such; rather, there is a situation from which the play
radiates into wider situations. This is not in itself entirely strange
for Soyinka. Even in *The Lion and the Jewel*, which seems to be
a long way off in technique from *Madmen and Specialists*, the
author had resorted to deepening and widening the scope of the
play through flashbacks. He uses this fluid approach increasingly
in later plays, particularly in *The Strong Breed* and *The Road*.
But in all those earlier plays the changes in time had been fairly
clearly signaled so that there was discernible a controlling
framework from which these flashbacks departed and to which
they returned. In *Madmen* the whole structure is far more fluid,
and there is continual fading back and forth so that time and
place become almost abstract. There are few definite references
to time, and even these only serve to blur the time system.

There is a similar abstraction of character. The villagers in
The Lion and the Jewel are firmly delineated and have a fixed
social entity from which they consciously, and with fair warning to the audience, elect to take part in a play-within-a-play.
Similarly, some characters in the control framework of *A Dance
of the Forests* double as characters in the Court of Mata Kharibu,
which is essentially a flashback. No such boundaries and signals
are given in *Madmen*. The characters are fluid and change back
and forth continually, requiring constant attention and interpretation from audience or reader. They start, in fact, by being
nearly abstract characters whose names and appearances invite
detachment rather than identification on the part of reader or
audience.

Although in some parts of the play Africa is faintly recalled,
this is Soyinka's most unlocalized play, the scenes being performed in a vague "down here" with constant references to "out
there" from which fearful deeds are reported. The names of
the characters strike no obviously associative chords—Goyi, Aaafa,
Bero, Iya Mate, Iya Agba,[19] and Si Bero—while others bear
representative labels rather than names—Blind Man, Cripple,
Priest, the Old Man. This tendency toward abstraction and an-
onymity invests the play with a strangeness, and effects a distanc-

ing of what goes on on the stage. Soyinka here closely approaches Brecht's alienation effect, and the atmosphere achieved by the practitioners of "Theater of the Absurd." Soyinka has, however, arrived here in his own time and in his own way, in a logical development of ideas and techniques which had been hinted at in earlier plays.

Not the least of the uses of this style of writing is its insulation from too particular references to times, places, and persons, a not undesirable advantage to writers in "sensitive" societies. It does have the addtional advantage of making the play even more universally applicable. It would need hardly any adaptation to fit into any particular society.

One way in which the play seems to differ from the plays of, say, Beckett and other practitioners of "Theater of the Absurd" is that though insulated from everyday reality, with *Madmen and Specialists* the connection with this reality is fairly readily made. With reasonable attention, the seemingly disjointed and seemingly illogical dialogue reveals a tough strand of its own internal logic running through, and although words seem to be batted about as meaningless counters, this itself is thematically significant; it is a representation of the verbiage which in real life is a mere smokescreen for the actions of the rulers of increasingly authoritarian societies in many parts of the world.

There are many themes in *Madmen*, but it seems that the central enveloping theme is the erosion of humanity in a well-organized, tightly controlled authoritarian society. The very appearance of the Mendicants portrays men as victims—as sufferers. These men, disabled or deformed, are victims of an undefined "blast," some sort of explosion, which had taken place "out there." This has reduced them to beggars who put on a macabre act—exaggerating their disabilities—to catch the pennies of passersby. But they also function ambiguously in the more active role of spies and secret agents of Bero the "Specialist" who is the symbol of the authority "out there." (The Mendicants have other roles, particularly as a kind of chorus.)

When the play opens, the Mendicants are engaged in a macabre game of dice, the stakes for which are parts of their already disabled bodies. Goyi, who has gambled away all his limbs and has become "just a rubber ball" as a result, insists on playing on, offering to use his mouth to throw the dice. The picture is of men eagerly, even greedily, enhancing their further ruin. As the

Blind Man fatalistically puts it, "Sooner or later we all eat
sand." This opening tableau can thus be taken as a miniature
representation of man in his world or, in the cryptic words of
the play, "The Creatures of As in the timeless parade"; man
in a pantomime of perpetual self-destructive folly. Man is both
sufferer and activator of his own suffering. The Mendicants have
similarly ambiguous roles throughout the play.

Si Bero, who is next introduced, industriously collects herbs
for her "Specialist" brother who is absent "out there." Her whole
life is wrapped up in her herb collection which is obviously a
symbolic occupation; it keeps her anchored to her humanity. In
her words to her brother, "I like to keep close to earth." Her
devotion to earth and humanity has brought her into an alliance
with the mysterious old women ("earth mothers") Iya Agba and
Iya Mate. These vague pointers to Iya's significance in the play
are enough to contrast her with the thing that her brother has
now become "out there."

Once, Bero's life too had been devoted to medicine; he had
been similarly tied to "earth" and humanity. He has now exchanged this humane existence for its very opposite. When his
sister ceremonially pours a libation of palm wine in front of
the doorstep on his return, he makes a chilling reference to the
less humane preoccupations of his new world "out there":
"We've wetted our good earth with something more potent than
that you know." His sister recoils from the implications of this
sinister hint with horror: "Not you. Neither you nor father. You
had nothing to do with it." But it becomes increasingly clear that
Bero is now committed to quite opposite principles from his
sister. Human blood rather than palm wine is now his customary
offering to the earth. For his sister, this is an abomination. This
is the central polarity of the play: the humane on the one hand,
represented by Si Bero and the earth mothers, and the inhumane
represented by Bero and the world "out there," an inhumanity
conveniently symbolized by the eating of human flesh.

Bero, whose return is the central event of the play, is revealed
as the jailer of his own father now imprisoned in his own house.
The Old Man has fallen ideologically foul of the regime in
which his son is a powerful figure. The father's crime is manifold,
with two or three aspects being prominent. He, apparently in
irony, gave the regime the name of its philosophy—"As"—which
the adherents adopted before they really understood what it or

the Old Man meant. One of the son's tasks now is to torture his father into revealing the real meaning of "As." The Old Man seems to have got the new men to face the full logic of their own inhumane actions; he tricked them into eating human flesh, on the ironic principle that all intelligent animals killed for food and that these inhumane rulers might as well save on meat by eating their victims—a grim piece of logic typical of the play. The Old Man thus made the new men face the full inhumanity of their regime, which they were otherwise too apt to cover in a smoke screen of words. The Old Man is also fleetingly but very significantly pictured as Socrates. His son obliquely suggests suicide to him by dropping some poison berries over the Old Man's head with these words: "If you ever get tired and you feel you need a nightcap like a certain ancient Greek you were so fond of quoting, just sink a handful of them in water." The Old Man has, like Socrates in the eyes of his accusers, been corrupting the youth by teaching them to think. (The youth are conveniently represented by the Mendicants in another of their numerous roles.) In a speech to Si Bero, Bero puts the case against their father thus:

Father's assignment was to help the wounded readjust to the pieces and remnants of their bodies. Physically. Teach them to make baskets if they still had fingers. To use their mouths to ply needles if they had none, or use it to sing if their vocal cords had not been shot away. Teach them to amuse themselves, make something of themselves. Instead he began to teach them to think, think THINK! Can you picture a more treacherous thing than to place a working mind in a mangled body?

(The passage, one of the comparatively few long speeches, is quoted at length because in addition to the point about the Old Man's "crime," it gives a picture of life "out there.")

Bero himself emerges as a cold-blooded technocrat totally devoid of humanity. His one remaining link with his human condition, and hence with any obligation to being humane, is his father. While the Old Man remains living, Bero cannot forget that he also is human. The Old Man therefore has to die in order to sever Bero's visible bond with humanity. The Old Man puts the point to Bero: "I am the last proof of the human in you. The last shadow. Shadows are tough things to be rid of. How does one prove he was never born of man? Of course you could kill

me. . . ." The logic of the Old Man's reasoning is demonstrated
when at the end of the play Bero shoots him. This is a further
step in his attempt to dehumanize himself. Since he is a symbol
of the technocratic regime "out there," this dehumanization is
characteristic of the whole regime. (Bero's growing alienation
from the humane is also seen in his renunciation of his earlier
humane profession, his lack of sympathy with his sister, and his
driving out of the earth mothers.)

Bero is dressed in military uniform and carries a swagger
stick and a gun, both of which he does not hesitate to use. These
and other hints suggest that he represents a military regime, a
suggestion compatible with the totalitarian nature of life "out
there." These military suggestions should not unnecessarily limit
the applicability of the play; it is relevant to all kinds of regimes
military or otherwise which are based on inhumanity and
repression.

Pessimistic though the play seems to be, there is always a
suggestion of the eventual futility of regimes like Bero's. They
are certainly grimly successful for a time and pile up against
themselves a horrible toll of victims. But even in the height
of their success they display a knowledge of their own precariousness. This is why they have to go on torturing and killing. This
is why they have to have spies. This is why Bero has to torture
information out of his father of the real meaning of "As." The
forces of life which such regimes violate have a way of presenting a silent, continuing threat. Bero and his crew live in constant
dread of this. This is what the Old Man points to when he defies
Bero to do his worst: "I recreate my tentacles so, cut away." In
spite of Bero's bluster, he knows that this is true. What little
hope there is in the ability of humanity to triumph is admittedly
buried under the physical realities of the repressive regime which
is for the time being all too successful, and the play cannot be
called really optimistic. The hope is too faint, but it is there.

As has been suggested, there is little dramatic action in the
play. All the action lies in the words which are very suggestive.
It is the words, continually fading away into new meanings,
elusive, slippery which keep the play alive. The very slipperi-
ness of words is significant. It is one of the themes of the play—
the total unreliability of manifestos, promises, laws, indeed all
that society is supposed to be based on. In this slippery world,
even breaches of faith can become manifestos. A good illus-

tration of this is the incident in which Bero forces his father to accept a cigarette when the Old Man prefers his pipe. Bero starts with an assertion: "I promised you the best of everything and this will prove to you what I mean." The "proof" turns out to be a refusal of the man's wish for his pipe. Bero then launches into a justification of his violation; indeed he exalts the violation into a creed. Toward the end of the speech, Soyinka introduces alliterative echoes which signal a preoccupation with the sounds of words rather than any meaning they might contain, a device which he uses frequently in the play:

Need and want. The overlap soon vanishes. Choice, particularity, what redundant self-deceptive notions. The wish to exercise a freedom of choice only creates an untidy existence. If the best is available then the exercise of a choice is not only unintelligent it is undignified. It is a childish form of greed. Insistence on a floppy old coat, a rickety old chair, a moth-eaten hat. . . . Is it sensible to cling desperately to bits of the bitter end of a run-down personality? To the creak of an old chair, the crack in a cup, a crock of an old servant, the crick in the bottle-neck of a man's declining years. . . .

The same technique of demonstrating the devaluation of words into mere sounds is seen in this exchange between father and son:

Bero: They were provided a Creed but they talked heresy. Same as you.
Old Man: Creed? Heresy? Bread, Pleurisy and what next? Will you try and speak some intelligible language?

Sometimes the echoes lead us, through association, from innocuous to sinister suggestions which help to give the play its insidious undertone of terror. In this next example the dialogue moves from the innocuous suggestions of "lamps" to grim suggestions of torture and death through electricity:

Old Man: A lamp has its uses.
Aaafa: So, electricity
Goyi: Bleeah! Election promises
Cripple: What we want is individual manifestoes
Aaafa: Manifesto for every freak? General Electric!
Old Man: Electrocutes. Electric chair. Electrodes on the nerve centres—your favourite pastime I believe? . . .

This seemingly disconnected dialogue (more typical than the long speeches of the play) is seen to be full of suggestion; broken election promises feature cheek by jowl with political torture. This technique of free association makes the range of suggestion of which the play is capable almost boundless. It is certainly a significant work exploiting new techniques, but it is consistent in its themes with Soyinka's earlier work. Once again the forces of life and the forces of death are shown in mortal opposition.

CHAPTER 3

Poetry

THE first separate collection of the poems of Wole Soyinka was published in 1967 by Methuen under the title *Idanre and Other Poems*. These poems had previously appeared in small clusters or singly in journals and anthologies including *Encounter, Ibadan, Black Orpheus,* Langston Hughes's *African Treasury,* Francess Ademola's *Reflections,* and Moore and Beier's *Modern Poetry from Africa.* Soyinka has featured since in other anthologies, including Donatus Nwoga's annotated anthology *West African Verse* (1968), and in 1969 Rex Collins Ltd. issued in a broadsheet, *Poems From Prison.*

Since Soyinka himself selected the poems for *Idanre and Other Poems* the collection gives a valuable clue to the poet's view of his own poems. Excluded are the light satirical poems "Telephone Conversation" and the twin poems "Two in London" which—particularly the former—had hugged the foreground of attention and established Soyinka almost exclusively in many minds as a writer of light satirical verse. The omission of these poems gently directs attention to the much greater part of his poetry, which is of quite another mood. On balance, Soyinka is not essentially a humorist—although even his graver poems are startlingly witty and sometimes grimly humorous—and his exclusion of his brilliant but on a general assessment, uncharacteristic "Telephone Conversation" was a shrewd authorial indication. It is well therefore to look at Soyinka's poetry using *Idanre and Other Poems* as the essential corpus. (Citations in this chapter will be to this volume.)

Soyinka emerges from this collection as a serious poet concerned with the grave issues which face him as a man first of all in his own country Nigeria, but eventually as a man living in the twentieth century. Because he objectifies the particular stimuli which give rise to the poems by using representative images, the poems have an independent existence from those stimuli, and they stand as art irrespective of them. It is there-

fore not necessary to pry too closely into biographical or historical events even when, as is often the case, the poems are expressions of intense personal feelings arising out of actual experiences. Often the poet saves the critic a good deal of trouble by
announcing the historical or other background of the poem in the
title, as in "Massacre, October '66," "To My First White Hairs,"
and others. His titles not only place many poems in this way
but often supply important keys to their meaning.

An appreciation of Soyinka's poetry depends primarily on a
sensitive realization of the significance of a well-organized system of images within each poem, and a willingness to follow
wherever the images lead. Very few writers in any age or tradition are better able to use words more suggestively than
Soyinka. In his ability to fuse a whole wealth of meaning into the
small compass of a poem he reminds one of the best of the
English metaphysical poets, particularly Donne and Marvell
and (although he is not usually grouped with them) of Shake-
speare.

I Imagery in "Massacre, October '66"

Although Soyinka is essentially neither a descriptive nor a
narrative poet, he is particularly sensitive to landscape—not
landscape in a pictorial sense, but as an informing environment
which supplies the essential images which ultimately *are* the
poems. As an introduction to the generalizations inevitable in
a work of this kind, a particular demonstration of Soyinka's
method will be given through a close examination of one of his
poems, "Massacre, October '66."

The title points directly to a particular historical event. The
poet gives the further information "Written in Tegel." The
poem's images, even without this information, announce through
"willows" the cold lake, "dying leaves," and "falling acorns"
that the setting is autumn in a northerly climate. But the information "Written in Tegel" is useful and helps to suggest a
richer meaning for the last stanza of the poem than might have
been easy to arrive at without it.

The northern landscape, as has been suggested, provides the
system of images for the poem which starts innocuously with a
location of the poet and a suggestion of his mood, the mood being
expressed through the same image of the lake which helps to

locate the poem: "Through stained-glass/ Fragments on the lake I sought to reach/ A mind at silt-bed. . . ." The poet is not only looking into a lake, he is looking into his own mind which is plunged in despair, and therefore is, in the image of the lake, "at silt-bed." This fusion of different objects or ideas through a single image is characteristic of Soyinka's work and is the main source of his compactness.

The second stanza continues the dual process—the physical description which at the same time suggests other meanings. That the poet's mind as well as his eye is engaged is suggested by his picture of the dying leaves which, defying the gardener's attempts to sweep them into orderly piles, "flew in seasoned scrolls/ lettering the wind. . . ." The dried curled autumnal ("seasoned") leaves suggest scrolls on which words are written which therefore inform the wind with wisdom—"lettering the wind." In what seems therefore to be a physical description we have intimations of deeper meanings.

The autumnal landscape also provides the acorns which the poet infuses with grave and sinister significance. As he treads on them, "each shell's detonation/ Aped the skull's uniqueness. . . ." Shells are, of course, primarily the covering of the acorns, but along with the "detonation" the word suggests more sinister shells, and all of a sudden the physical treading on shells suggests the crunch of human skulls, the violation of human life, which is what the poem is all about. The shape and the sound of the acorns underfoot have been economically turned to graver purpose.

The acorns are exploited further; they are the favored food of hogs, and they fall in such numbers that they remind the poet of heads which are being as wantonly cropped in his own country which he has left temporarily. This attempt to match acorns with heads and to compare their massive fall to the killings in his own country is the "sharper reckoning" in the first line of the fourth stanza:

> Came sharper reckoning—
> This favoured food of hogs cannot number high
> As heads still harshly crop to whirlwinds
> I have briefly fled.

The linking of human heads with the favored food of hogs deftly suggests the devaluation of human life which is implied in the wanton killings. (Hogs are particularly despised in the area where the killings take place, an idea exploited more fully in stanza 8.) The image of an untimely harvest also underlines the wantonness and the waste of the killings. (The harvest image as will be seen is one of Soyinka's most frequently used images.) The harvest being premature—the result of "whirlwinds"—spells famine, a period of barrenness and deprivation in the future.

The mind boggles at all this and seeks refuge from the contemplation of this terrible waste of life; it takes temporary refuge in the externals of the autumn landscape. But as more acorns fall, Soyinka's mind goes back to the terrible events (in stanza 7). The victims of the slaughter have been rendered as silent as the acorns, but they once laughed; they had been human, and in being human—in being able to laugh at the same things as those who killed them—not strangers. The idea which is expressed tentatively here (stanza 7)—"They are not strangers all"— is stated even more finally in stanza 8—"not strangers any." (It is almost redundant to state here that those who were massacred were "strangers" to the area in which the killings took place.) The grim irony of the fact that the killings took place in an area dominated by Islam, an area whose commonest greeting involved "peace," and which shunned "unholy" acts like the eating of pork; this irony is the burden of stanza 8.

The last stanza has the surface look of an apology for using an alien landscape as the basis of a poem about his own country, but the landscape offers a particularly apt message. This "alien" land—Tegel (one now sees the value of this piece of information) —is an area in Berlin which under Hitler had seen the flourishing of a racial myth revolting for its exclusiveness. The borrowing of this landscape has special significance in the context of a slaughtering of "strangers"—those who do not belong:

> I borrow seasons of an alien land
> In brotherhood of ill, pride of race around me
> Strewn in sunlit shards. I borrow alien lands
> To stay the season of the mind.

The poet is in fact surrounded by the ruins (shards) of the Herrenvolk myth, in the name of which millions had been slaughtered for not belonging. The poet's own land becomes linked "in brotherhood of ill" with the alien land. (There is a suggestion of the poet's own pride being also in ruins about him.)

The selection of an "alien" set of images, the distancing of the events which this provides, saves the mind from collapsing under the strain of the actual events.

I suggest that not just here, but everywhere in his poetry, Soyinka's use of images provides him with the means of distancing the primary object, event, or experience which gives rise to the poem, and enables him to produce a work of art instead of a chronicle of events. "Massacre, October '66" is by this means far more than a historical record. It is a network of suggestive images sensitively arranged to suggest the essence of the massacre and its terrible consequences. It is a moral presentation of a historical fact.

The poems in *Idanre and Other Poems* are grouped under general thematic headings, and apart from this one poem which is taken out of its place, it is convenient to follow these groupings in an examination of the poems.

II *"of the road"*

The first group is headed "of the road." All of the poems are vaguely connected by the fact that they are based on experiences obtained while traveling (by road or air) or events which, like the death of Segun Awolowo in a car crash, took place on the road. The poems are not all of the same mood. The opening poem, "Dawn," celebrates the dawn as it is seen by someone who has been driving through the night. Although a number of physical objects appear in the poem, it is not primarily a photographic description. It seems to attempt to capture the essence, the spirit of the dawn—a time of day which often in Soyinka's poetry represents hope. (In "Death in the Dawn" this hope becomes ironical in that dawn provides the setting for death.)

As the dawn breaks, the tall palm tree is the first object that becomes visible—first, its spiky fronds "piercing" the air. The palm is endowed with a conscious pride in its position, almost like an athlete glorying in his achievement—"As one who bore the pollen highest." The red fruit of the palm becomes "Blood drops in the air." Some of Soyinka's images vaguely suggest a human figure gaily even coquettishly attired: "above/ The even belt of tasssels, above/ Coarse leaf teasing on the waist." The entry of the sun is portrayed in terms suggestive of human action. It

comes like a Tarquin, first stealing in—representing the gradual-
ness of the first approach of dawn—then erupting into action:
"The lone intruder, tearing wide/ The chaste hide of the
sky. . . ." This is rape indeed which is echoed by the disarray
implied in "Night-spread in tatters. . . ." (Tarquin's rape of
Lucrece is strongly suggested here.) The last stanza delicately
suggests the worship with which dawn is greeted. Not only do
the words "celebration" and "rites" suggest this, but the blood-
red kernels of the palm become an apt sacrificial offering to a
god who is himself "aflame." In the end, we have something like
the character of the dawn (rather than a photographic picture
of it) through images which suggest not only how the dawn
comes, but what it means.

It is on this ironic counterpane that the central event of the
next poem, "Death in the Dawn," takes place. Dawn is represented as a time of hope, but hope tinged with fear. Men rise
from their beds, quench their lamps, take up their burdens,
and make for the markets through the early morning mist; uncertain mortals peer into the future through folk augury and
hope that through propitiation of the gods they may avoid disaster. Underneath all this, the road, like a beast of prey, lies
in wait. All this is evoked through a series of interlocking
images:

> This soft kindling, soft receding breeds
> Racing joys and apprehensions for
> A naked day, burdened hulks retract,
> Stoop to the mist in faceless throng
> To wake the silent markets—swift
> Processions on grey byways. . . .

Neither the accidental killing of the cock (imaged as a vain
sacrifice—"futile" rite) nor the prayers of a fond mother—"child/
May you never walk/ When the road waits famished"—are of any
avail, however. The crash takes place, and as in other places in
his work, Soyinka captures the terrible and sudden transformation
from life to death. Here the dominant element is one of surprise as man (not just *a* man) becomes trapped in his own
invention:

> Brother,
> Silenced in the startled hug of

> Your invention—is this mocked grimace
> This closed contortion—I?

Soyinka succeeds in generalizing the particular through his use of images. The placing of "Death in the Dawn" after "Dawn," which is a celebration of the promise of dawn, is not without a touch of irony. Within the second poem itself there is a suggestion of fatalism—a suggestion that man's fate is independent of his attempts to propitiate the gods. The die seems to be cast in spite of prayers and propitiation.

Dawn (the time of day) connects "Around us dawning" with the poems which have gone before; it also is connected by the theme of traveling, though this time the traveling is not by road but by plane. Soyinka manages to convey the ambiguous nature of the plane itself; it is a creation—it was "fashioned"—but once created it takes on a being of its own; it becomes a proud, majestic, beast of prey: "This beast was fashioned well; it prowls/ The rare selective heights/ And spurns companionship with bird." The irony goes further, for even the creator, man himself, becomes the victim of his own creation. He yields his will to the machine: "Passive martyrs to the will of rotors." Indeed "martyrs" introduces a sequence of accompanying images which further indicate how close the plane in its pride is to its fall (and its contents with it—the "martyrs"). It takes only "an alien mote" in the machine to bring the whole thing down—"when/ Death make a quick descent. . . ." This proud machine in its vulnerability becomes "a carbuncle" and the mountain peaks potential "lances" to prick it open. Thus man in his machine is poised between triumph and disaster. The plane is further cut down to size as its false dawns pale into insignificance with the coming of the true dawn. In the darkness the plane had with its trails produced

> a linear flare, of dawns,
> —the incandescent
> Onrush.

This false dawn which the plane produces is nothing to the "power" of the sun when it "explodes" in the last stanza. The last stanza itself works on two levels, a further meaning being suggested by "dessication" which glances at the burned-out remains of a crash, reinforced by "explodes" even though in the

primary meaning it is the sun that explodes; in the context it is
difficult not to apply the explosion to the vulnerable airplane
as well.

"Luo Plains" yields its meaning less readily than some of the
other poems but is ultimately no less suggestive. Some of the
suggestions which can be derived from the images may perhaps not have been intended by the poet. The setting as the
title announces is Kenya and thus the landscape is made up of
objects from the area: egrets, lakes, the animal at the water hole,
spears, cowherds, the cactus, and the eagle. However, these are
used not just as an evocation of a physical landscape. The dawn,
for example, which is central to the meaning of the poem, is a
more significant event than the start of a new twenty-four-hour
day. It is the beginning of a new era, something as significant
as the coming of independence. This central event is treated in
the third section of the poem:

> That dawn
> Her eyes were tipped with sunset spears
> Seasons' quills upon her parchment, yet
> The hidden lake of her
>
> Forgives!

A physical dawn, and a physical lake had been introduced in
the preceding section, but here the dawn is more momentous.
It is a dawn which had been preceded by fighting—"sunset
spears." The sharpness of "spears" is echoed in "quills," although
primarily they are the pens with which the momentous docu-
ment, "the parchment," is signed. (The parchment seems to
confirm the idea of independence.) The achievement which is
confirmed by the signing of the parchment has been achieved
through fighting, but in spite of this, the country forgives her
foes. The isolation of "Forgives!" and the use of the mark of
exclamation suggest the massiveness of what is to be forgiven
as well as (or is this reading too much?) a certain incredulity
that such massive forgiveness is even possible. The last section
reinforces the idea of the enormity of what has to be forgiven
with images like "red sunset spears" and "reeds of poison." All
these are thoughts which are inspired by a mind dwelling on
a landscape (during an airplane flight) which suggests deeper
thoughts. The process by which this poem comes about is quite

similar to the processes which produced "Massacre" which had been treated earlier.

"In Memory of Segun Awolowo," which ends this section, arises from the death in a car crash of a friend of the poet. The personal nature of the loss is indicated by the use of "my" in "this fresh plunder/ Of my youth." The untimely death of the victim is imaged as an untimely harvest (a favorite Soyinka image): "For him who fell among reapers/ Who forestall the harvest. . . ." The familiar figure of the anthropomorphic road bent on plunder reappears, but this time the road is already glutted with plunder (and hence did not need this particular victim) so he "retched" on his latest victim. The drama of death itself is captured in the opening lines of the poem:

> For him who was
> Lifted on tar sprays
> And gravel rains
>
> In metallic timbres
> Harder than milestone heart

The end of the poem attributes crashes of this kind to the whims of Ogun; attempts to seek other causes—blaming shifting earth—are vain. The suggestion seems to be that we really cannot explain why a young man is suddenly selected to die in his prime in this way. It is the whim of the god. The figure Ogun, the embodiment of both the creative and the destructive essence, occupies a prominent place in Soyinka's artistic and critical writing.[1] That the god is also prone to caprice is evident in his devastation of his own people of Ire in the poem "Idanre." Ogun is also the god of the road by whose caprice men die on the road. This resolution of this particular poem is neither satisfactory nor comforting because there can be no explaining away the waste involved in such a tragedy.

III "lone figure"

"The Dreamer" introduces a figure which frequently appears in Soyinka's work, namely, the lonely inspired man in society who sees what others cannot see, and who, because he does not fit comfortably into the society's pattern, is martyred. Eman in *The Strong Breed* whom this figure particularly resembles—he too is martyred, high on a tree—is one such figure. The soldier

Mulieru in *A Dance of the Forests* is another such martyr to the society he tries to save, as is Sekoni, the engineer in *The Interpreters.* In the poem "Idanre," while all men await the promise of the harvest and the blessing of the god in passive hope, only the poet dares to make the perilous pilgrimage to watch the god in his agony. Although "For Fajuyi" is not included in the section "lone figure" he too earns death (and later glory) by walking the lonely path by which society, in spite of itself, could possibly be saved:

> What goals for pilgrim feet
> But to a dearth of wills
> To hills and terraces of gods
> Echoes for voices, shadows for the lonely feet.

"The Dreamer" deliberately evokes memories of Christ's crucifixion. Indeed, if the dreamer is not Christ himself, he is a Christ figure. His crucifixion as one of three, his crown of thorns, the nails on his flesh, myrrh (one of the presents of the wise men), as well as his words—not just the "words" on the cross but all his preaching—are all evoked in the first stanza:

> Higher than trees a cryptic crown
> Lord of the rebel three
> Thorns lay on a sleep of down
> And myrrh; a mesh
> of nails, of flesh
> And words that flowered free.

The influence of the martyred man is pictured in the images of growth; the seed falls to the earth and dies but germinates and grows, spreading its influence over the seas. This happens to the martyr here in the last stanza which also economically defines the nature of his influence with words suggestive of Christian church organization and ritual—"see," "thrones," and "incense." Incense on the sea at the end also suggests the great spread of the religion:

> The burden bowed the boughs to earth
> A girdle for the sea
> And bitter pods gave voices birth
> A ring of stones
> And throes and thrones
> And incense on the sea.

This poem is the first of the few in the collection in which Soyinka employs rhyme (*abaccb*) as well as alliteration and other echoic poetic techniques. All these make the poem one of his most deliberately musical. The last three lines are particularly so with "And" separating stones, throes, thrones slowing up a line which through the repeated closed "O" sound seems to suggest the inexorable spread of influence which the lexical meanings of words imply.

"The Hunchback of Dugbe" illustrates Soyinka's ability to transform the mundane into art. Poetry has come out of car crashes, so why not out of lonely lunatics? The hunchback is one of the unfortunate madmen who, detached from their surrounding countrymen, walk their lonely demented way all over tropical Africa. What happens in the poem and to the hunchback does not become clear until (as with a number of Soyinka's poems) we see the significance of subtle changes in the tense. The poem opens, and goes on for five sections, in the past tense. "I wondered"—"The devil came." After the advent of the devil the tense changes to the present: "the world/ Spins on his spine, in still illusion. . . ." This is in fact the historic present. It describes the gruesome death of the man (run over by a cement mixer truck) who had "By day, stooped at public drains/ Intense at bath or washing cotton holes," and whose night paths had been a mystery. In spite of his death, however, the hunchback walks on, visiting his old haunts in Dugbe in his ghostly nudity:

> At night he prowls, a cask
> Of silence; on his lone matrix
> Pigeon eggs of light dance in and out
> Of dark, and he walks in motley.

The imagery of the poem is worth close attention—without which in fact it remains a puzzle. The presentation of the hunchback in the three opening sections is straightforward enough. His clothes, more holes than cloth, are "cotton holes." His own twisted malformed figure—twisted body on crooked legs—is suggested in "An ant's blown load upon/ A child's entangled scrawl. . . ." The dramatic moment is the running over of the hunchback by the cement mixer, pictured here as the devil's own vehicle. The mixing chamber of the vehicle becomes the devil's "vast creation egg." The bowl is egg-shaped and with its cement mixture is a source of building and hence of creation. The egg is a fortunate linking image. Of course here it does not create, but Soyinka imbues it with a positive significance which justifies the suggestion. The hunchback is transfigured into the plane of existence where physical beauty and ugliness are meaningless. He is, in fact, released from his grotesque body into a different existence. This is an act of creation (or at least of transformation).

> Not in disdain, but in truth immune
> From song or terror, taxi turns
> And sale fuss of the mad, beyond
> Ugliness or beauty, whom thought-sealing
> Solemnly transfigures—the world
> Spins on his spine, in still illusion.

He now prowls in silent nudity, but this time seemingly riding on a ghostly mixer—"lone matrix." This reading of the poem, although the product of many readings, is rather tentative and is open to objections. It has been pointed out to me for instance that the figure at the end of the poem with its emphasized masculinity (but, I suggest, not necessarily virility) is far too vivid for a ghostly figure. There is some point in this. What happened when "The devil came" is crucial to an interpretation, and to me the images in the crucial stanzas are confusing. There is enough wit apparent in the poem as a whole, however, to make one return to it again and again for a way through its apparent obscurity in parts. Sometimes Soyinka has the fascination of an intellectual crossword puzzle.

"The Last Lamp" is a poem in which the original object has been totally transformed into new images. As is not unusual, the poem starts with a physical image; a delicate image of a weak light in the surrounding darkness: "A pale incision in the skin of night. . . ." The image of "incision" is sustained by "bled" which suggests ebbing life, and reinforces the idea of the precarious state of the light. In the context of this image of bleeding to death, "Dye" (surely a pun) and shroud fall into place, underlining the imminent death of the flickering light, and gently introducing the human object for which the light seems to be a symbol. This is confirmed by "Her" in the second stanza. All the associations here are of an old and frail woman—she is described through her shadow—which now gathers close about her and is "a lying depth"—a phrase which already points to the length of the old woman laid out as a corpse. The phrase "generations patient stoop" suggests both the great age of the woman as well as her figure, bent with age, as she goes in and out (the doorways are also crooked) and as she patiently waits out her time in spite of her troubles ("peace denied"). The tense changes in the second line of the last stanza—"She *was* a vespers' valediction, lit/ Within deserted ribs...."—suggesting that the light has now gone out. She has come to the end of her long day, but she *was* the valediction which suggests that not only she, but an era died with her.

"Easter" produces yet another lone figure—the man who distils the wisdom of the surrounding world, but who has to do this in isolation. The poem is organized around the idea of the distillation of perfume from frangipane flowers. It starts with the evocation of a scene in which, in the stillness of a particular evening—"This"—the poet smells the perfume of the frangipanes. The evocation of the scene and thoughts arising from it continues for four stanzas with other objects from the surrounding environment brought in. The central image (and with it the main thread of the poem) returns with the frangipanes in the fourth stanza. These flowers are weak and fall easy victims to the wind: "These pink frangipanes of Easter crop/ Eager to the wind"; yet they are vital ingredients with which to counteract the deep-seated decay of earth. For this purpose they have to be gathered and distilled. But the odds against this halting or counteracting of the earth's decay being successfully accomplished are very heavy indeed. There is only "ONE" bough, and there are millions waiting for the balm—the whole earth is rotten —"One bough to slake the millions? Decay/ Caulks the earth's centre; spurned we pluck/ Bleached petals for the dreamer's lair." The business of redemption has to be undertaken by the "spurned," solitary "dreamer" in his "lair"—away from the mass of men. (I am inclined to treat this particular "we" as a majestic "we." It is essentially singular. "Dreamer's" is singular too, and in the next stanza, the pronoun becomes "I.") The dreamer, then, armed with the petals he has saved, proceeds to his lair for the distillation: "Borne passive on this gift, wound-splashes/ From the wind-scavenger, sap-fragrance for/ A heady brew, I rode my winged ass and raged—" Once again the change of tense from present to past introduces a note of historicity: "I rode my winged ass and raged." This is the poet in his state of

possession, but the source of the imagery—Christ's triumphal
entry into Jerusalem on Palm Sunday—is unmistakable. It con-
firms faint references to the passion—too weak to lead to confi-
dent assertions by themselves—"palm" and "crown" in stanza 4.
Thus we have a recurrence of the Christ figure—the martyr to
his own society—the man who is spurned but who nevertheless
has the perfume with which to halt the decay of the society
which rejects him. This is the heart of the poem. The emphasis
is on the passion, on the agony of isolation, not on the glorious
resurrection which the title "Easter" would lead one to expect.
The Easter lies in the fact that the solitary does collect some
frangipanes, does distill some perfume, and does rage. His words,
like the words of the dreamer in the opening poem of this
section, might yet bear fruit, but in the uncertainty of human
affairs, only might. At the end of the poem the children like the
indifferent society unconcernedly continue their wonted activities: "As children wove frond yellow from the palm/ Plucked
at the core, within the spadix heart. . . ."

IV   *"of birth and death"*

The section "of birth and death" is delicately graduated. It
starts with "Koko Oloro," a children's propitiation chant playful
in rhythm and tone, which by its very artlessness conveys the
helplessness of man. The section continues through poems arising from the birth and death of children to one on the first reminders of old age, "To My First White Hairs" and ends with
"Post Mortem," which pictures the dead man on a slab unknow-
ingly yielding the secrets of life to the investigating fingers of the
pathologist.

"Dedication" invokes a blessing on the newly born infant in
language which is based on that used by elders in ceremonies
like that of *komoja* when the child is formally recognized as
having been born and is introduced to the world. There is a
proliferation of images from the environment in a fervent prayer
for a full life for the infant. From its proverbial opening to the
fossiled sands at the end, the poem proliferates with images
from the surrounding environment, all made to yield significance in particular wishes for the child. The gecko falls unhurt
from the perilous heights of the hut's rafters to the hardness of the
dung floor beneath; so (runs the implication) in the inevitable

falls the child is bound to encounter she will receive no hurt.
"Earth will not share the rafter's envy: dung floors/ Break, not the
gecko's slight skin, but its fall." The yam, the springs, the baobab,
the earth all combine in a wish for life—secure, continuing, productive. Like "peat," a symbol of unhurried development and
long life, the child is to grow free under the benevolent influences of nature—rain, the sun's shadow, and the night's protection. Nor is the child to grow into a spineless butt. Symbolic
items like pepper, palm wine, and the various preparations used
in the child's toilet combine to invoke a full, healthy, productive
life, all leading to the final wish that her life may leave a permanent influence: "Yield man tides like the sea/ And ebbing, leave
a meaning on the fossilled sands. . . ."

The light, heady atmosphere of buoyant hope in "Dedication"
is chilled by the hopeless grief and lamentation of the mother
of a stillborn child in "A Cry in the Night"—another ironical
sequence. The posture of grief—the mother beating her head on
the floor—provides the opening:

> As who would break
> Earth, grief
> In savage pounding, moulds
> Her forehead where she kneels.

In an uncharacteristic use of the pathetic fallacy the poet isolates the mother from any source of comfort as even the stars
desert her: "No stars caress her keening/ The sky recedes from
pain. . . ." (Soyinka has reached in "keening" for an unusual Irish
word. A "keen" is an Irish funeral song accompanied with wail-
ing; hence to "keen" is to wail or lament bitterly for the dead.)
Apart from the very apt "keening," the selection of "caress"
here is extremely sensitive; it suggests the warm comfort of
which the mother is here deprived, and thus dramatizes her
loneliness. This loneliness is further underlined at the end of
the poem. It is the mother herself who buries her child "in haste"
as custom demands. Her physical pain, as well as her mental
anguish, is fully evoked:

> Such tender stalk is earthed
> In haste. A stricken snake, she drags
> Across the gulf, re-enters to the retch
> Of grieving wombs. Night harshly folds her
> Broken as her after birth.

The image of earthing the stalk here ironically echoes the earthing of the living yam tuber in "Dedication." This earthing is a
mocking of that earlier hope. The mother in her state of pain and
physical exhaustion—"Broken"—becomes a wounded snake whose
slow painful progress is highlighted by "drags" while the pain
makes the journey seem endless—"gulf." The bleeding which is
inevitable in birth but which is accepted in a joyful birth is now
mere revolting waste expressed by "retch." Once again Soyinka's
extraordinary ability in selecting the apt word to produce the
appropriate set of suggestions has made art of an almost intoler-
able human situation.

"A First Deathday" has a similar inspiration—the death of a
child, this time on her first birthday—but it is of a different tone
altogether. Here the grief has been got over, and there is an
attempt to distil some meaning from the event: "Grief has long
receded, yet the wonder/ Stays. . . ." The third stanza contains
the attempt to rationalize the experience and is the burden of
the poem:

> Knowledge as this in growth's diffusion
> Thins, till shrouds are torn from swaddlings.
> She was not one more veil, dark across
> The secret; Folasade ran bridal to the Spouse
> Wise to fore-planning—bear witness, Time
> To my young will, in this last breath
> Of mockery.

At the end of "In Memory of Segun Awolowo," Soyinka had
attempted a similar rationalizing of the experience attributing
the death to the whim of Ogun. That attempt seems almost
cursory in the face of this more elaborate one. Here it is suggested
that at birth we bring with us a certain knowledge which "thins"
as we remain in this world—"in growth's diffusion." (This as the
basis of the rationalization reminds one of Wordsworth's "trailing clouds of glory.") By living, Folasade would thus have dissipated this knowledge; but by assuming her shroud almost as
soon as she sheds her swaddlings, she preserved this knowledge
undissipated. In her case there was no "veil" across the
"secret" (which life would have provided). Hers was a wise,
deliberate act—"fore-planning" and "will" emphasize this. The
deliberateness of the child's act—her conscious will—is seen (in
a different mood) also in "Abiku." Folasade's was also a joyful

act as she "ran bridal to the Spouse." In her joy at meeting her spouse, the incidental "mockery" of the hopes of her parents (hopes beautifully elaborated in "Dedication") is inconsequential. The Spouse (capital "S") is the creator to whom the child returns and who seems also to be an embodiment of knowledge. The poem rests on the idea of the continuum of life from pre-existence through life on earth to a continuing existence after death.

The idea of a purer form of being—called knowledge—which is dissipated by life and growth on earth, recurs in "For the Piper Daughters" where, in contrast to the purity, innocence, and openness of childhood, age is characterized by a false appearance, deceit, and lies. The children are enjoined therefore not to grow old in this way, but to retain the qualities of their childhood "I would you,/ Thus, never old. . . ." The poem turns on this contrast between the purity of childhood and the guilt of age. Not only is there a contrast portrayed, for example, in the open-handed "largesse" of childhood contrasted with the miserly "slits" of age, but age actually poses a threat to youth which must be resisted. The children have to be armed against the lascivious wiles of the false priest and (like the child in "Dedication" using her pepper) must take extreme action against him. The double-edged image of the rose is exploited here:

> The rose, you know, is thorned. And if
> The cozening priest would slay you, panting
> How your cheeks are rudded like the . . .
> Riddle him with lethal pips!

The opposition is total; the priest's intentions are murderous—"slay." The children's protection must also be total; the pips of the rose must become deadly—"lethal." Fortunately, every good beautiful creation comes with its protection (and its price):

> To the date
>   A stone
> The linnet
>   Height
> Pearls
>   Depth and the clam

The rose is similarly "thorned" and its pips potentially lethal. The wish for a free, healthy, fruitful life under the influence of nature for the children is similar to that of "Dedication."

The death of a child portrayed as a positive act of its will has been noticed in "A First Deathday." The Abiku child, who comes to plague its mother with a temporary stay only to return to her mischievous kind in the other world soon after, is a figure in Yoruba belief. In "Abiku" Soyinka emphasizes the callous wilfulness of such a child who haughtily scorns the pleas, the sacrifices, the ritual scarrings and all other efforts calculated to "earth" her, to make her stay: "Yams do not sprout in amulets/ To earth Abiku's limbs...." (The earthed yam image has been noticed before in "Dedication" and ironically in "A Cry in The Night.") The continuity of the Abiku cycle as well as its terrible linking of birth and death is suggested (as do "shrouds" and "swaddlings" in the different context of "A First Deathday") by the juxtaposition of "mounds" (graves) and "yolk" (the source of life): "In silence of webs, Abiku moans, shaping/ Mounds from the yolk...."

"To My First White Hairs" is a fairly lighthearted greeting of the first signs of age—lighthearted, but still not averting the eyes from the direction to which they point—decrepitude and death. There is a progression in the suggestions of the images of the last line and a half of the poem: "knit me webs of winter sagehood,/ nightcap, and the fungoid sequins of a crown...." The "three white hairs" of stanza three give way to the prospect of "winter sagehood," "winter" suggesting the total whiteness through the image of snow, but "sagehood" introducing the idea of the wisdom that comes with it. "Nightcap" takes the idea further into debility and death, while "crown" (even though somewhat deflated by "fungoid") looks hopefully beyond life toward higher things.

This easily leads on to "Post-Mortem," which also has a half-mocking approach to a grim subject. Soyinka deliberately cuts man down to size with this picture of the body on the slab. Man is reduced in the opening lines to the status of beer, being only another possible item in the stock of a refrigerator. The process of deflation is more explicit in

> his mouth was cotton-filled, his man-pike
> shrunk to sub-soil grub
>
> his head was hollowed and his brain
> on scales.

It is to this unprepossessing object that man has shrunk, and
yet (glory be!) even this object has some use; it may yet, ironically, teach through the investigating fingers of the pathologist
"how not to die." The wit of the poet was never more apparent.
Soyinka's wit is just as evident in his treatment of this rather
grim subject as it is in the lighter and earlier "Telephone Conversation."

V   *"for women"*

The poems in this section are linked by the fact that a woman
is part of the stimulation for each one, but the section consists
of poems of varying moods. It is another series of variations on
a theme. The first two poems, "Song: Deserted Markets" and
"Psalm," are as different as two poems can be; they are, in fact,
opposites. The image of the seed or grain as the source of growth
is the dominating image in both poems. In the first, the seed is to
be frustrated; it is not to be allowed to grow; therefore it is
deprived of moisture:

> My soul shall be dry
> In an ebony grain
> Keep it from sprouting
> In a stranger's pain.

Thus the seed is not tended; it is gobbled up—greedily devoured
—hence destroyed by the white bird: "A white bird she comes/
And gobbles the grain. . . ." Consequently there is no harvest:
"And the dew leaves no mark/ Where my head has lain. . . ."
The fate of the seed in "Psalm' is more fortunate; it has
been tended and has reached a happy harvest. All the images
suggest fullness, mature growth, and harvest: "the seeds have
ripened fast my love/ and the milk is straining at the pods. . . ."
The straining pods—the full breasts of the delivering mother—
are in contrast to the "Moon-breasts of pain" of the "stranger" of
"Song: Deserted Markets." "Moon" reinforces the racial identification of "white" in "white bird," in contrast to "ebony."
"Stranger" is used in both poems, but in "Song" it typifies an
alien spirit with whom there is minimal spiritual contact, while
"stranger" in "Psalm"—"The Stranger life"—means new life,
referring to the child which is the harvest of the grain. The harvest is triumphantly celebrated at the end of the poem as a
manifestation of the mystery of the continuing cycle of life:

> and a mystery
> of pulses and the stranger life
> comes to harvest and release
> the germ and life exegesis
> inspiration of your genesis.

The encounter in "Song" is a dry, commercial unproductive one
whose negative nature is shown up when compared with the
fruitfulness of "Psalm."

"Her Joy is Wild" also looks forward to birth: "This is the
last-born; give me/ A joyful womb to bind. . . ." But the emphasis
is on the ecstatic, joyous abandon of the woman in the sexual
act itself. Unlike the restraint of the central event in "Song,"
there is to be no withholding or frustration of the seed, no
lingering at the edge of the experience. The invitation is to total
involvement with the kernel—the heart of the fruit, not the rind:
"Your strong teeth will weaken/ If you nibble at the rind. . . ."
The wild joy is dramatized by the "skeins of hair" plucked
unconsciously by the woman at the height of her joyous delirium.
The man's willing response expresses the total mutuality of
the act: "—and I denied her/ Nothing, maimed on her vision
of the blind. . . ." These three poems, then, form a three-part
variation of the theme of sex and its fulfillment (or the absence
of it). The restraints of "Song" are prompted by racial over-
tones—the "ebony grain" and the "white bird"—which contribute
to an absence of the full mutuality (there is a positive suggestion
of pain) and produce a very different kind of experience from
that of the other two poems.

"Black Singer" conveys the reaction of the poet to the song
of a black female singer. One way into the heart of the poem
is through an examination of the images in the second stanza:

> A votive vase, her throat
> Poured many souls as one; how dark
> The wine became the night.

The singer's throat is a "votive vase"—a sacrificial vessel—out of
which "poured" her song (the wine) which is not only her song
but also a representative cry, since what was poured out was
also "many souls as one." The selection of "souls" introduces
the idea of the depths of man's being. Thus the singer's song
springs out of, and expresses the deep feelings of a whole host
of people for whom she speaks through her song. The darkness

of the "Song" (wine) expresses the background of suffering of the souls for whom the singer speaks. It evokes the whole history of suffering of the Negro people. This is confirmed by the suggestions in stanzas 4 and 5:

> Dark, lady
> Dark in token of the deeper wounds
>
> Full again of promises
> Of the deep and silent wounds
> Of cruel phases of the darksome wine

The darkness of the lady's complexion merges with the darkness of her song and with the darkness of the night: "how dark/ The wine became the night. . . ." The singer is no opera prima donna but a "soul" singer, a "natural": Fleshed from out disjointed, out from/ The sidewalk hurt of sirens. . . ." As the lonely envoy of her race, the darkness—the whole history of suffering of her race—comes pouring out as a sacrificial offering out of the "votive vase" that is her throat.

"Bringer of Peace" presents the qualities of a woman whose tactful influence has a steadying effect on the persona who speaks in the poem. The imagery of the poem has to be followed with some care. The woman's influence, symbolized by light rain, does not act in total opposition to the fire; its influence is more subtle. By questioning out, testing his rage (rather than by opposing it with equal force), she acts as a touchstone—tests the quality of his rage: "You come as light rain, not to quench/ But question out the pride of fire. . . ." This fact is again portrayed in the last stanza as "This cunning sift of mild aggression." In the second stanza she is again characterized through the action of light rain, as a soothing influence. The effect of "deft" to qualify intrusions is to show the woman, though gentle, to be adroit and deliberate in her gentleness. Thus, her gentle rain produces a "hiss." A hiss is a sound of anger, but it is also a sign of the loss of heat in fire, hence a sign of cooling (of the poet's rage). Both meanings are relevant here. Even in the act of raging (in reaction to the gentle rain), the rage is stilled.

The third stanza reveals the man's rage as a protection—"they hold the beast at bay"—with which he represses the instinctive reaction which is to "howl" when he is hurt. The man's rage then

is consciously built up, as "accomplishments" suggests. The rage
is also a cover for the frustrations of his spiritual imprisonment:

> Yet fires that hold the beast at bay
> Inclose, with all accomplishments of rage
> The inborn howl, proud lacerations
> Futile vaults at high bounds of the pit.

This is the rage which the "bringer of peace" prods, identifies,
evaluates, and stills subtly, even imperceptibly:

> This cunning sift of mild aggression, then
> Is your rain, a tacit lie of stillness
> A smile to test the python's throes, a touch
> To bring the bowstring's nerve to rest.

"To One, In Labour" yokes the process of gestation to the
social organization of ants. Thus stated, the yoking might sound
farfetched and overingenious. Indeed, on early readings the
ideas seem to be uneasily yoked together. The opening of the
poem—the first two stanzas and the first line of the third—presents the analogical image which is to be applied in the second
half: the industry of the ants in building and in ministering to the
queen ant. The most important detail in this social organization
of the ants is contained in the lines: "Some to labour some to
yield/ A queen her labour. . . ." It is the function of some of the
ants to make the queen ant pregnant. Elementary biological
knowledge supplies the information which is employed a little
later in stanza 3, that male ants die after mating: the "dead
lovers" and "master masons," having done their work, have now
departed. The anthill now forms the poet's symbol for the
process of gestation in which only one sperm is required to fer-
tilize a single ovum for the process of gestation to start. The
superfluous sperm are also "dead lovers" and "departed . . .
master masons":

> And I think
> Gestation is a Queen insealed
> In the cathedral heart, dead lovers round
> Her nave of life.

"Cathedral heart" and the related architectural term "nave"
echo the building (and laboring) image first introduced through
the industry of the ant "architects." In "master masons," "mud

spires," "colonnades," "shrines," and "catacombs" the architectural image reverberates throughout the poem.

The process of gestation then resolves itself eventually into a union of two entities—"Desolate/Wonder of you and me." The sperm and the ovum are microscopic echoes of the human "you and me" who start the process. Once the seed is sown the process takes place—"Insealed/ In the cathedral heart"—in the womb, now a "shrine of pain" (it was once a shrine of love and pleasure). As the "lethal arc"—the pregnant womb—contracts, and the secretions flow, the process of labor begins. The poem has moved full cycle from the "regurgitations" of the ants to the secretions of the one in labor—an ingenious exercise of the poet's wit, demonstrated by his extremely sharp eye for analogies.

The seed which comes to fruition in "To One, In Labour" is sown during one highly charged explosive moment in a compulsive instinctive act, when the deep drives take control, and conscious attempts to strangle the seed give way. The seeds assert themselves with an independent will of their own at this charged moment: "and strangled seeds/ Unleashed, exult. . . ." These are the seeds of life which in the opening lines of the poem "In Paths of Rain" write lives on moments:

> In paths of rain, in rock grooves, may
> These rare instants of wild-fox-fires
> Write on moments, lives.

(Here as elsewhere syntactical analysis helps to reveal the meaning of complex passages: "These rare . . . fox-fires" is the subject of "write" and "lives" is the object. "On moments" is adverbial. In stanza 2 "strangled seeds" is subject to "exult." In stanza 5 "still-traps" is a verb to which "sable oil" is subject, and "a straining thunderhead" is object.) Even this early stanza suggests the momentary nature of the essential process which is vividly symbolized in succeeding stanzas. But the momentary act is produced in a social context and thus breeds a train of consequences of an entirely different nature from the act itself. The act is instinctive; marriage is social. The act may be begun and ended in total mutuality; the vistas are clean:

> Clean vistas—
> Flecked mica after rain, plankton in antimony
> Off rain-washed shores.

But the end of the poem suggests that the mutuality of the instinctive act may produce quite other results in the larger context of the society. The suggestions of this section are very compactly presented—the earlier part of the poem is more expansive; the structure itself is suggestive. Everything is bright, the poem suggests,

> Till the chronicle of severance
> Gold spelling, lantern sanctuaries around
> Birth-point, and chapter. . . .
>
> Ground skins of the unshelled
>   hand over hand of fire
> As kernel's freak communion
>   windpools in the ash of palm.

The "severance" in contrast to the mutuality implied in the earlier stanzas takes place in an atmosphere suggestive of church and ritual: "lantern sanctuaries" and "chapter." In this context "gold spelling" would suggest a book with gold lettering—for example, the prayer book. "Birth-point" suggests an advanced stage of pregnancy. Altogether, the suggestion is of a marriage required by society because of a pregnancy. The two "unshelled" (ungloved) hands are here in a "freak communion" in contrast to the more natural communion portrayed earlier. The glitter of "mica after rain," the fruitful suggestions of "plankton in antimony" have become a more barren "windpools in the ash of palm. . . ." This union in fact has, ironically, become "the chronicle of severance." The poem separates the instinctive physical act from the social rigidities which often complicate it. It is an important variation to the theme of this section.

The occurrence of "By Little Loving" in the section "for women" tends to inhibit a liberal interpretation of the poem. In my reading "loving" suggests something more general than feelings for an individual; it suggests rather a total commitment to life. The poem seems to suggest a period ("once," i.e., not any more) in the subject's life when, by holding back from a full commitment to life he sought to avoid the agony which total commitment can bring. In the first stanza this idea is focused on love—he withdraws from a total commitment to love—but the other stanzas put this into perspective since the withdrawal is from other aspects of life as well.

The first stanza represents the subject's attempt to insulate himself from love, love being equated with the life-giving forces. The imagery suggests a retreat into a dead, unproductive state. This is clear in the following lines:

> a bank of bleached
> Shells kept the floods at bay—once
> By little wisdom, sought the welcome drought.

The qualifier "bleached" suggests dryness, which is later reinforced by "drought." "Shells" in the context suggests the mere outside covering of the organism (which presumably is now dead, the shells being now used as a barricade). So that the total state portrayed is a dead unproductive barrenness. The retreat into this state is from the irrigating "floods" which had they not been barred— kept at bay—would have brought life. In the subject's perverse state, this drought was welcome; the choice of death for life was deliberate. That he recovered from this perverse state (which is further elaborated in most of the poem) is suggested briefly in the last stanza when the forces of life assert themselves from within, instinctively:

> They kept vigil long, the winds and the stilled
> Night rage, and the tread of waters proved a lie
> Bursting from within. . . .

The details of the poet's flight are portrayed in different images. What seems to have been a retreat from the liberal use of his imagination is suggested in

> I kept
> My feet from flowered paths. I bared
> The night of stealth, watched thwarted
> Winds beat cycles, deafened as a crypt. . . .

By refusing to see what was going on around him he found a false comfort at the still center "off the ruptured wheel/of blood." The cosiness of his position at the center of the wheel gave him the illusion that he had discovered permanent truth through this retreat—"by little yearning." ("Little" here has the force of a negative.) He had had enough of the agony of involvement: "the wear/ Of pulses, stretch of flesh hunger hourly hurled. . . ." He found a temporary refuge in a naïve position, refusing to reason himself into a personal position. He had ac-

cepted "hate," for example, in this way. He had, in fact, in the
suggestions of the last stanza, been on the path of eternal death
(without benefit of the phoenix's powers of self-reincarnation),
but mercifully the instincts he had tried to suppress asserted
themselves, and he was spiritually redeemed.

For me, then, the poem has meanings far larger and more significant than its place in this section would seem to suggest. A
denial of love in the restricted sense of personal feelings for a
person would have been only one symptom of what was in fact
a state near to spiritual death; a total denial of his real self, and
a mock-existence in a false comfort.

VI   *"grey seasons"*

Insofar as "I Think It Rains" pictures a state in which rain,
instead of liberating, restricts and imprisons, it has something
thematically in common with "By Little Loving" in the previous
section. "Rain," as has been hinted earlier, in Soyinka's symbolism represents a life-giving force. When it comes it should dis-
sipate the forces of death. This is what is asserted in the first
stanza as the true function of rain. The tense of "rains"—the
present of custom or habit—is crucial here, and makes the first
stanza a statement of a general truth, in contrast to the past
tense "saw" in the second stanza which gives that stanza a particular historicity. The first describes what rain *does* or ought to
do while the second describes what it *did* (or failed to do) on
a particular occasion:

> I think it rains
> That tongues may loosen from the parch
> Uncleave roof tops of the mouth, hang
> Heavy with knowledge.
>
> I saw it raise
> The sudden cloud, from ashes. Settling
> They joined in a ring of grey; within,
> The circling spirit

Contrary to expectations, instead of liberating, the ashes, react-
ing abnormally to the rain, have imprisoned the human spirit
which circles helpless within the restraining circle. The "closures
of the mind" in stanza 3, then, are (surprisingly) the results of
rain which, as needs to be reiterated, is normally liberating. It

has brought negation. In the fourth stanza, it "beats" on wings (hence restricting flight) and suppresses desires.

In stanza 5 there seems to be a separation of the poet from others which is signaled by "my" in contrast to the plurals "us" and "our" earlier. The rain has had a quite different effect on him. The raindrops which look soft but really are quite powerful have eroded his topsoil and exposed the "crouching rocks" beneath

> Rain reeds, practised in
> The grace of yielding, yet unbending
> From afar, this your conjugation with my earth,
> Bears crouching rocks.

"Crouching" has the suggestions of ready to pounce. The effect of rain on the poet is therefore liberating. It releases latent energies in him.

One needs, for total satisfaction from this poem, a correlative for "rain." Freedom in a general way, or independence, more particularly, would seem to serve the purpose. This freedom, instead of liberating the mind, brings an odd closing which in some ways parallels the denial of life that is the subject of "By Little Loving."

The image of a restricting circle—"a ring of grey"—within which the spirit is enclosed, central to "I Think It Rains," is more explicit in "Prisoner" where the subject is also in a mental prison: "And time conquest/ Bound him helpless to each grey essence...." By the end of the poem, the "walls" are set and the prisoner is "closed" in sadness. The accumulations of gray which set into the prison walls are not sudden formulations. They form and harden imperceptibly from the gray wisps of the "threads" and catch the subject unawares when the "sudden seizure" of the last stanza occurs.

A change in tense in the middle of the poem is once again significant. The present tenses of the first two stanzas—"Curl," "breed," "begin"—convey general truths; the change to a measure of particularity comes in the third stanza. The general truth seems to be that the prisons of thought and position in which men find themselves are not sudden outgrowths, just as, the imagery suggests, heads do not suddenly turn gray. The single threads "compulsive of the hour" presage the "wise grey temples" of

later years. Intimation of the later positions come even in the
wild years of youth, well before the febrile years.

The images in the third stanza suggest wild youth, particularly nimbleness and agility over rugged territory—"even amidst
the/ Crag and gorge, the leap and night tremors. . . ." Even here,
"intimations came," but the potsherd stayed; preserved a whole-
ness. (It is stricken in the next stanza.)

The end of the second stanza introduces the dramatic event
at the end of which there are changes. The alienation between
erstwhile companions is evident

> For that far companion,
> Made sudden stranger when the wind slacked
> And the centre fell, grief.

(The "threnody"—song of lamentation—had been heard in the
middle of the storm.) The "potsherd" which had "stayed" up to
now, "lay disconsolate." "He" (the far companion—far because
alienated) suddenly found himself in a position of alienation.
But the "intimations" had been there all along; they did not
come with the storm which only revealed what had always been
latent. Time had now conquered. The walls had set; the wisps
had become gray temples; the prisoner was now truly encircled.
All the earlier suggestions unite to form the final prison in the
last stanza:

> He knew only
> Sudden seizure. And time conquest
> Bound him helpless to each grey essence.
> Nothing remained if pains and longings
> Once, once set the walls; sadness
> Closed him, rootless, lacking cause.

It is worth mentioning that in one version the poem ends with
the line "Bound him helpless to each grey essence."[2] The poet
prefers the longer version in his own collection, but the poem
is essentially complete in the shorter version. The prisoner is
already bound to the gray essences; he is a prisoner. The addi-
tional three lines of the longer version reinforce the idea of a
walled prison, but in addition suggest a possible definition of the
gray essences by the phrase "pains and longings." If these "pains
and longings" are identified with the individual wisps and threads
earlier, then they suggest something like the individual's own

struggles and ambitions, his daily struggle to reconcile personal goals and possibilities. These are the hourly threads which eventually build the gray temples. (The pun on temples—edifices and heads—should not be missed.) My personal preference is for the shorter version without the particular suggestions of "pains and longings."

If this poem had been written after the Nigerian Civil War, it would have been easy to see in the "Sandstorm" the war which suddenly revealed erstwhile friends in opposed attitudes on either side of the cause. But it appeared long before—in Francess Ademola's *Reflections* (1962)—and is thus saved from this narrower interpretation. Th possibility of such an interpretation, however, is a good illustration of one of the paramount qualities of Soyinka's poetry. Because it is couched in images and is thus removed from particular incidents—because the poetry is not essentially "narrative"—it achieves a generality of application which transcends the particular local application. This is one reason why his poems are likely to survive any incidents from which they might have sprung. It is also this characteristic that makes Soyinka far more than a local poet, either in space or in time.

The theme of "Season" is summarized by its epigrammatic opening: "Rust is ripeness." By juxtaposing "rust" (a symbol of age and decay) with "ripeness"—maturity and full growth—Soyinka suggests the cycle by which growth leads to death and a new beginning of the cycle. The poem employs the present and the past tenses to convey subtle shifts of emphasis. The present tense of "Rust is Ripeness" indicates general truths. The section "And we loved" refers to a particular past time, that is, youth. With "now" in the second section of the poem we come to the present state of "we," namely the evening of life when

> we
> Awaiting rust on tassels, draw
> Long shadows from the dusk.

The rhythm of birth, growth, and decay—"Laden stalks/ Ride the germ's decay"—is also suggested in the passing of afternoon (which is the time setting for the "spliced phrases . . . rasps in the wind," etc.) into the evening implicit in the "now" passage. Soyinka tends to see human history both individual and collective in terms of cycles. Thus, even rust can be promising, for it points to the decay of the germ, which brings new life. The poem therefore ends in hope, a hope couched in irony:

> Laden stalks
> Ride the germ's decay—we await
> The promise of the rust.

"Night" is one of the few Soyinka poems in which the physical image remains at the center of the poem rather than an applied situation which arises from it. It is an evocation of the effect of night on the poet, with a call at the end for deliverance from "night children" which haunt the earth.

"Fado Singer" is a tribute to a performer in the genre. (Fado is a type of popular Portuguese song and dance with a guitar accompaniment.) The poem is a record of the poet's reaction to the sadness of the song. The singer had captured the grief of the gods as in a net spun from the strings of her instrument "Your net is spun of sitar strings/ To hold the grief of the gods...." These same strings later intensify in the imagery and become sutures (surgical stitches). The image of pain which is implied in "sutures," a pain which is the effect of the song, runs through the whole poem. By the end of the poem, the poet longs for relief from the grief induced by the song.

VII *"October 1966"*

Exact dates when things happened are not as important to a study of Soyinka's poetry as they would be in a study of the work of a chronicle poet. This is true even when one is considering poems springing from actual events as those falling under the general title "October 1966." This date points roughly to its central event, the killings of "Strangers" in northern Nigeria which took place during September and October, 1966. (The first killings were reported on September 29.) By October, 1966, Lieutenant Colonel Francis Adekule Fajuyi, military governor of the Western Region of Nigeria, had been seized and killed. He and General Ironsi were abducted on July 29. Even a poem as pointedly dated as "Ikeja, Friday Four O'Clock" does not depend on the precise date on which a particular truckload of soldiers was seen, since the poem is really about the waste and negation of life that war (not just the Nigerian war) brings.

All the poems spring from experiences during the troubled

period from about October, 1966, to the months leading to Civil War. These were obviously traumatic events for the poet—he was to spend most of the war in detention—and the miracle is that he can write about them with the artistic detachment which these poems display. Together with "Poems From Prison," written while the poet was actually in detention, they are an excellent demonstration of Soyinka's ability to distance the immediate object or event through imagery. This ability enables him to portray dreadful and devastating events as well as intimately personal ones without prosiness or sentimentality. The poem "For Fajuyi," for example, is a self-contained whole which yields its meaning wthout any knowledge of who Fajuyi was. (This knowledge of course gives a further bonus.) Like *A Dance of the Forests*, a grim warning of how easily man could destroy himself and transform his potential for life into negative channels, these poems gaze with horror at man, the victim of his own power, substituting death for life.

"Ikeja, Friday Four O'Clock" is as particular as a title can be, pinpointing as it does both place and time. The poem is obviously inspired by a truckload of soldiers bound for battle action. However, interest does not lie in their particularity but in the waste of life that they represent: "They were but gourds for earth to drink therefrom. . . ." The perversion by which the contents of the gourds are uselessly spilt when they should have been put to better use is echoed throughout the poem. The sacrifice was unnecessary; the gods did not ask for it; the altars (hence the priests) were false: "Unbidden offering on the lie of altars. . . ." The familiar images of the bad harvest ("crop of wrath") and the perverted feast reappear. The resulting revulsion is signaled by "retch" in "No feast but the eternal retch of human surfeit. . . ." The echo of the injunction from "The Feeding of the Five Thousand"—Gather up the fragments that nothing be wasted —dramatizes the irony. The needs of the country require that "nought be wasted," yet the wine is being poured into the ground, and human lives are being devoured and retched in a degrading orgy of waste. The life-giving "loaves" of the miracle of the loaves and fishes have been travestied by "loaves of lead."

In all this the soldiers appear as worthless sacrificial victims, so close to their sacrifice that they are even now "a mirage of breath and form." These particular soldiers are Nigerian (except for the title, however, the poem does not stress this), but they represent the sacrifices of false priests to false gods in numerous wars all over the world, throughout history. Relieved of its particular title, the poem becomes a universal picture of the waste that is war. The substitution of death for life, "loaves of lead" for loaves of bread, is a constant preoccupation in Soyinka's work.

The image of the bad harvest reappears in "Harvest of Hate." (The death of Segun Awolowo is also portrayed as an untimely harvest—he is a victim of "reapers who forestall the harvest.") Here the harvest is equally untimely and on a more massive scale. The songs of harvest, the joys of harvest, the whole hope and promise of harvest have been frustrated:

> There has been such a crop in time of growing
> Such tuneless noises when we longed for sighs
> Alone of petals, for muted swell of wine-buds
> In August rains, and singing in green spaces.

The waste is itemized in earlier stanzas; its massiveness is signaled by the untimely death of the sun and by a spoiling of the fruits of the harvest:

> So now the sun moves to die at mid-morning
> And laughter wilts on the lips of wine
> The fronds of palm are savaged to a bristle
> And rashes break on kernelled oil. . . .

There is a grim reminder that this "forfeit of old abductions" is to be paid in human lives, the lives of a new generation:

> The child dares flames his fathers lit
> And in the briefness of too bright flares
> Shrivels a heritage of blighted futures.

The image of destruction by fire which runs throughout portrays both the physical painfulness of the process and the totality of the waste.

In "Massacre October '66" (a complementary analysis of this poem appears earlier, pp. 110-13), the poet uses the imagery of the environment in which he finds himself at the time of the massacres—"seasons of an alien land." This not only has a therapeutic value for him—the distancing stays his mind from collapsing under the enormity of the event—but it has a similar value for the reader too. The alien images of autumn provide an artistic machinery through which the uninvolved reader can be brought to the heart of the experience. The use of the surrounding landscape is an illustration of Soyinka's ability to start from where he is, to express his meaning by the means immediately available to him. He always harnesses the environment to his purpose. Tegel (a residential section of Berlin) in Autumn is made to do service as the environment through which the horror of the October massacres in the poet's own country is portrayed. There is an astonishingly intelligent fusion of the falling and fallen acorns with the more gruesome image of heads being cropped and crushed at home: "I trod on acorns; each shell's detonation/ Aped the skull's uniqueness...." The transformation of the acorns is effected through the pun on "shells"— the protective covering of acorns, and cannon shells— which leads naturally to "detonation" of both types of shells which are then fused with the human skulls in the next line. The mind of the poet in the depths of depression had been similarly fused with the very bottom of the lake in the opening stanza. He had been looking both into the lake and into his own depressed mind: "I sought to reach/ A mind at silt bed...." It is through such yoking of the objects of the surrounding landscape with what was happening at home that Soyinka makes his point. The acorns also provide the vehicle through which he expresses the devaluation of human life which the massacres imply. Acorns are plentiful and cheap—"The oak rains a hundred more"—and are "This favoured food of hogs...." There is an implied cheapening of human heads which are being equally indiscriminately harvested in his own country: "As heads still harshly crop to whirlwinds/ I have briefly fled." The hog idea is to be given even more ironical significance in the penultimate stanza when Soyinka uses it to dramatize the irony of the fact that the massacres took place in a land whose everyday greetings involved the idea of peace and where in observance of religious teaching the eating of pork was taboo. The juxtaposition of the observance of such teachings with the "desecration" of human life provides an eloquent comment:

> Whose desecration mocks the word
> Of peace—*salaam aleikun*—not strangers any
> Brain of thousands pressed asleep to pig fodder—
> Shun pork the unholy—cries the priest.

The immediate environment is made to yield one more vital significance in the last stanza which is much more than an apology for using an alien environment to portray Nigerian events. The environment could not have been more apt in one sense. Not only acorns lie around him in this alien land, but "pride of race around me/ Strewn in sunlit shards. . . ." We recall that this was the home of the Herrenvolk theory which because of its exclusiveness led to the massacre of millions. The parallel is instructive. Perhaps this too helps to stay the mind— it had happened before and man had survived.

War as a travesty of life is implicit in "Civilian and Soldier" where the civilian is on the side of life and the soldier on the side of death. The soldier is a victim of his situation and training. His finger itches instinctively for the trigger on which all his training is focused. His instinctive reactions are toward inflicting death. This is his "plight." The sudden appearance of a civilian in his area therefore sets in train an instinctive reaction which brings the civilian within an eyelash of death. The irony is that behind the seeming certainty of the soldier's outward reactions is fear and uncertainty. The poet sees the "plight" of the soldier:

> and when
> You brought the gun to bear on me, and death
> Twitched me gently in the eye, your plight
> And all of you came clear to me.

(Apart from anything else, the poise of these lines, particularly the phrase "and death/ Twitched me gently in the eye," illustrate Soyinka's control.) The soldier is engaged in his trade of death and has nothing to offer but bullets. The civilian's revenge therefore (when the opportunity is favorable) is to bombard the soldier with life-giving items:

> No hesitation then
> But I shall shoot you clean and fair
> With meat and bread, a gourd of wine
> A bunch of breasts from either arm. . . .

The poem is more than an indictment of a single soldier; it is a confrontation between the processes of life and death. The soldier's position is all the more pathetic because he too is caught in spite of himself. His is a "plight" of being involved in death, a "plight" brought about by forces much larger than himself. The larger questions which determine peace or war are all beyond him. His answer to the question at the end of the poem would no doubt have been "no": "do you friend, even now, know/ What it is all about?"

The tribute "For Fajuyi" arises from the fact that Fajuyi tried to find out what it was all about. He was a soldier, but he is also that recurrent figure in Soyinka's work—the lonely seeker, the man who sacrifices himself for the good of his society, whose "lonely feat" must be offered for the redemption of his society. "The Dreamer," the lonely poet in "Idanre," Eman in *The Swamp Dwellers* all trod the lone path Fajuyi trod:

> What goals for pilgrim feet
> But to a dearth of wills
> To hills and terraces of gods
> Echoes for voices, shadows for the lonely feat. . . .

The irony here as elsewhere where these lonely figures appear is that, while they fall, "Weeds triumph."

In all the terrible events which gave rise to these poems, the poet retained an objectivity both as an artist and as a Nigerian. He was able to see above "us" and "them." For many people— and again this is implicit in a number of poems—only the super- ficialities were visible, and their joys as well as their sorrows were strictly partisan. Only the few—the lonely pilgrims—have the imagination to suffer with "enemy" as well as "friend," to see into the essence of things, and recognize essential humanity. In "Malediction" Soyinka rains terrible curses on one who re- joiced, no doubt at one of the disasters to "them" rather than to "us."

> Unsexed, your lips
> have framed a life curse
> shouting joy where all
> the human world
> shared in grief's humility.

For this denial of life she is cursed to a life in which death appears where most she looks for life, and laughter when sorrow is more appropriate to her condition. Her bier is thus to be impiously hooted to its grave by her inebriated children, even as she has laughed in an hour of human grief:

that their throats laugh Amen
on your bier, and carousing hooves
raise dust to desecrate dust—Amen.

VIII *"Idanre"*

"Idanre," Soyinka's longest poem, was written in 1965 and
published in 1967. In it the poet has used the Yoruba mythological background as the vehicle for ideas which would be familiar
to one who has read the poems and the plays. The very figure
of the poet on a lonely pilgrimage is a recurring Soyinka image.
While the generality of men keep the safety of earth awaiting in
passive hope the blessing of the god at harvest time, the poet
dares to make the lonely pilgrimage and intrude on the god's
preharvest agony:

> I walked upon a deserted night before
> The gathering of Harvest, companion at a god's
> Pre-banquet   (p. 81)

It is to those only who dare to gaze alone on the naked truth
that the hills "yield their secrets." "Idanre" is a record both of the
poet's pilgrimage and of the secrets which it yields.

This framework allows the poet to introduce many of his
favorite themes—the waste of war, the consequences of free will,
the celebration of individuality, death on the roads, man's
potential as well as his proneness to self-destruction, the nature
of the god Ogun—all themes which reappear elsewhere, but
which in "Idanre" are given a new form and unity.

Section I of the poem, "deluge," sets the scene at the start of
the pilgrimage. The storm which precedes the walk is described
in terms which evoke the presences of the gods behind it—
Sango the god of lightning and electricity ("the axe-handed
one"), and Ogun, the god of iron whose metallic cables bear
Sango's electricity to earth—"He catches Sango in his three-
fingered hand/ And runs him down to earth. . . ." And more
specifically later: "One speeds his captive bolts on filaments/
Spun of another's forge." The storm is now over, and only the
occasional flashes of lightning making patterns with the clouds,
and the dripping leaves carry evidence of its fierceness. But
terrible though the storm may be it is also the promise of harvest. The harvest image, as will be seen later, is central to

"Idanre."[3] Men as well as the land welcome this rain without question (only the poet dares further into "secrets hidden from him"):

> And no one speaks of secrets in this land
> Only, that the skin be bared to welcome rain
> And earth prepare, that seeds may swell
> And roots take flesh within her, and men
> Wake naked into harvest-tide.   (p. 62)

Soyinka uses the present tense here, a tense which he often uses to express not only what is current but additionally what recurs or is permanent. (The subtle alteration of tenses within a poem is important in the interpretation of all Soyinka's poetry. It is certainly important in a long poem like "Idanre" where there are frequent changes of tense and hence of significance.) There is thus (because of the use of the present tense in their portrayal) something both in the storm and in the dependence of man on the gods for the harvest that is archetypal—a permanent pattern. When the actual pilgrimage starts in the second stanza of section II of the poem, the historic past tense is used. Ogun's arrival in what is a recurring pattern—"again"—is portrayed with the present tense, as distinct from the particular pilgrimage in which the poet joins. First the ritual reappearance:

> He comes who scrapes no earthdung from his feet
> He comes again in Harvest, the first of reapers
> Night is our tryst when sounds are clear
> And silences ring pure tones as the pause
> Of iron bells.   (p. 62)

For the particular historic walk with which the poem is concerned, the tense changes:

> We walked
> Silently across a haze of corn, and Ogun
> Teased his ears with tassels, his footprints
> Future furrows for the giant root.   (p. 64)

The pilgrimage in the company of a god is preluded by a communion with another human being, "the wine-girl." This brief communion with the wine-girl is the poet's last link with his own kind. She is not only human, but woman, and her femininity is highlighted:

                                        vapours   rose
             From sodden bitumen and snaked within
             Her wrap of indigo, her navel misted over
             A sloe bared from the fruit

             Darkness veiled her little hills poised
             Twin nights against the night, pensive points
             In the leer of lightning, etc. . . .   (p. 63)

Earlier her "womb" had echoed in human terms the rhythm of
harvest so important in the symbolism of the poem. There is
something archetypal about her too. In his notes to the poem
Soyinka endows her with three personalities. Apart from her
primary personality as the wine-girl, she is "Also Oya, once the
wife of Ogun, laterly of Sango. . . . Also a dead girl killed in a
motor accident." In the poem itself she is the principle of
womanhood; the eternal mother; the human counterpart of
Mother Earth, and thus similarly responsive to the elements.
As she stands in the rain she too like the earth earlier receives
its benevolent influence, her skin bared: "the thatch/ Ran rivu-
lets between her breasts. . . ." In her elevated role she provides
an anchor for the poet in his lonely and hazardous walk among
gods and spirits. He is "earthed" to her:

             And to one whose feet were wreathed
             In dark vapours from earth's cooling pitch
             I earth my being, she who has felt rain's probing
             Vines on night's lamp-post priestess at fresh shrines
             Sacred leaf whose hollow gathers rains   (p. 66)

His mind twice returns to the wine-girl during his walk with
the god. As an ordinary human being she would avoid the
hills; she would be prepared to wait "incurious" for the harvest.
She cannot understand why the poet would seek the hills at
such a time. In her query she is a representative of the mass:
"what then are you? At such hour/ Why seek what on the hills?"
Her query underlines the poet's isolation and the incomprehension
with which the society receives his words and actions—even
those meant for their benefit. His separation from the wine-
girl is symbolic of his separateness from the society he serves.
But he is still "earthed" to her and the society. His relationship
is thus fraught with ambiguity. It is this underlying ambiguity

that tends to make the lonely poet the victim of his own society which he seeks to save.

The walk with the god takes us through familiar paths at first. The landscape bears the marks of man's inventiveness—high-tension cables symbolizing the union of Sango and Ogun and motor roads strewn with the wrecks of motor vehicles, offerings to the demanding god Ogun. Men have quarried the earth, refined the ores, harnessed electricity, and created marvelous artifacts which in turn destroy them. The irony of this situation intrigues Soyinka as the recurrence of this theme in his works show. This irony reflects an ambiguity in the nature of the god Ogun who is both creator and destroyer. It is he who inspires the worker in metals; it is also he who demands the sacrifice of the road. Men are both Ogun's protégés as well as his victims:

> And we
> Have honeycombed beneath the hills worked red earth
> Of energies, quarrying rare and urgent ores and paid
> With wrecks of last year's suppers, paved his roads
> With shells, intestines of breathless bones—
> Ogun is a demanding god.　(p. 64)

As the poem continues, the irony builds up as not only the wonderful artifacts of man are reduced to "Playthings for children, shades/ For browsing goats" but as man himself, the lord of creation, is reduced to a mere ingredient in the cycle of growth, and his brain, the spring of all his cleverness, is equated with sheep's excrement after his own invention has claimed him as a victim in a car crash:

> growth is greener where
> Rich blood has spilt; brain and marrow make
> Fat manure with sheep's excrement.　(p. 65)

But man is more than body: the dead, humiliated in body, rise in essence and join the ranks of the departed ancestors to protect the living and receive their tribute. The cycle, like the cycle of the harvest, is never-ending:

> They rose,
> The dead whom fruit and oil await
> On doorstep shrine and road, their lips

> Moist from the first flakes of harvest rain—
> Even gods remember dues.   (p. 65)

The continuing cycle is represented by various symbols in Soyinka's work. Later in this same poem he uses the image of the snake swallowing its own tail—well known in Yoruba iconography—and the "Mobius Strip" to represent this principle of cyclical continuity or evolution:

> Evolution of the self-devouring snake to spatials
> Now in symbol, banked loop of the "Mobius Strip"
> And interlock of re-creative rings, one surface
> Yet full comb of angles, uni-plane, yet sensuous with
> Complexities of mind and motion.   (p. 83)

The walk is interrupted by a reversion into the poet's childhood and the deliriums and nightmares of his dreams. The reason for the occurrence of this passage here is not immediately clear and has to be worked out. In an inspired moment during the walk, the poet's sensibilities have become heightened, and he has seen and felt the presences of the dead:

> Suffused in new powers of the night, my skin
> Grew light with eyes; I watched them drift away
> To join the gathering presences.   (p. 65)

Two stanzas later the childhood visions are introduced with the lines:

> Vast grows the counterpane of night since innocence
> Of apolcalyptic skies, when thunderous shields clashed
> Across the heights, when bulls leapt cloud humps and
> Thunders opened chasms end to end of fire:
> The sky a slate of scoured lettering.

The change of tense from "grows" to "clashed," "leapt," "opened," is significant. The growth of the sky since childhood "innocence" is both a present fact and a continuing experience. The fantasies of childhood had been a confused jumble of the oddments of formal education—the nursery rhyme cow jumping over the moon is just perceptible in "bulls leapt cloud humps"—and Yoruba lore; later a "gaunt *ogboni*," vaults off on a zebra's back. The point of all this is that the experiences are jumbled and unorganized. Since then the experiences of the night have become vaster. This particular night, for example, has already yielded an important enlargement of the counterpane of night in the vision of Ogun and the presences. More enlargement is to come by the end of the experience which the poem describes.

The second section of the poem ends with an even further retreat into time, back into fossil time, to the creation of order out of chaos at the beginning, when Ogun, the creator started the "loop"—the word is significant—of time.

> The night glowed violent about his head
> He reached a large hand to tension wires
> And plucked a string; earth was a surreal bowl
> Of sounds and mystic timbres, his fingers
> Drew warring elements to a union of being
>
> And taught the veins to dance, of earth of rock
> Of tree, sky, of fire and rain, of flesh of man
> And woman. Ogun is the god that ventures first
> His path one loop of time, one iron coil
> Earth's broken rings are healed.   (p. 68)

This picture of Ogun as the creator, the first venturer and indeed at this point in time the only god, links up with section III in which Ogun, now one of many, grieves over the splitting of the single essence by Atunda's act of smashing the godhead with a boulder—a piece of mythology of which Soyinka makes significant use.

> Union they had known until the Boulder
> Rolling down the hill of the Beginning
> Shred the kernel to a million lights.

The sudden creation of a multiple godhead is in contrast to the tortuous path of man's own evolution which is partly fated and partly self-willed: "Man's passage, pre-ordained, self-ordered winds/In reconstruction. . . ." The present signals the continuing nature of the winding path. The search for an undefined goal continues: "And the monolith of man searches still/ A blind hunger in the road's belly. . . ." Ogun's own pilgrimage (as has been seen earlier) is recurrent. His words make this clear:

> *This road have I trodden in a time beyond*
> *Memory of fallen leaves, beyond*
> *Thread of fossil on the slate, yet I must*
> *This way again.*   (p. 69)

The poet follows the god, shrouded by night and the suggestive rock complexes of the hill, as Ogun once more sought "the season's absolution."

The relationship between Ogun and men has been seen as being ambiguous. Although man is a creation of the god, he is able to influence his creator even against the creator's better judgment. The men of Ire broke his resolve to separate himself from men once he had hewn a path to earth—itself a reflection of the god's ambiguous nature—and prevailed on him to be their king. The language suggests the persuasiveness of the men of Ire who as representatives of human kind manifest another facet of man's uncanny abilities from which he not only benefits but also suffers. The men of Ire drag the god down by their persuasive arts:

> But Ire
> Laid skilled siege to divine withdrawal. Alas
> For diplomatic arts, the Elders of Ire prevailed;
> He descended, and they crowned him king.   (p. 71)

The cost to the men of Ire—more dramatically portrayed in section V—is dreadful. They had enlisted the aid of ultimate force which, once they have enlisted it, they cannot control:

> O let heaven loose the bolts
> Of last season's dam for him to lave his fingers
> Merely, and in the heady line of blood
> Vultures drown.   (p. 71)

This is the potential that men have sought to harness for their own petty ends. The harvest they reap is proportionately bloody. Men harness ultimate force at their peril: "Who brings a god to supper, guard him well/ And set his place with a long bamboo pole..." (p. 72).

The poem here speaks eloquently outside its immediate context in comment on the almost unimaginable capacity in the hands of man—he is able to harness the god himself. Yet man has only his own puny selfish will to control this force. His use of the force, then, is often perverse and self-destructive because his will is not equal in magnanimity to the magnitude of his material strength.

> We do not burn the woods to trap
> A squirrel; we do not ask the mountain's
> Aid to crack a walnut.   (p. 73)

Yet in defiance of man's own proverbial wisdom, this is what the men of Ire did; this is what men always do. The consequences of the men of Ire's invoking of absolute force is dramatized in Ogun's "day of error" when the "lust-blind god" destroys friend and foe alike. Soyinka describes the physical terror of the god's blind rampage in a picture of matching terror. The god dwarfs everyone around him, symbolizing the disproportionate character of the unleashed force:

> Tall he rises to the hills
> His head a rain-cloud has eclipsed the sun
> His nostrils blow visible
>
> Exhalations as twin-flues through clouds
>
>   ✿   ✿   ✿
>
> His sword an outer crescent of the sun
> No eye can follow it, no breath draws
> In wake of burning vapour. . . .   (pp. 74-75)

Having portrayed the god with the aid of elemental parallels, the only terms which would do—rain clouds, the sun, burning vapors, and so on—Soyinka reduces the scale to portray the consequences to man. He chooses the familiar domestic image of a harvest—a bad harvest:

> There are falling ears of corn
> And ripe melons tumble from the heads
> Of noisy women, crying
>
> Lust-blind god, gore-drunk Hunter
> Monster deity, you destroy your men!   (p. 75)

The cost of the devastation is here given in human terms through the image of a reversal of the normal harvest. Confusion replaces order; the songs are turned to wails; the god drinks blood, the blood of his own men, for wine. As the god warms to his work he becomes in turn a butcher and a cannibal. The god who had been so susceptible to the "diplomatic arts" of men is now "deafened" to their helpless cries. He does not discriminate (any more than does a nuclear bomb):

> their cry
> For partial succour brought a total hand
> That smothered life in crimson plains
> With too much answering.

As the poet watched the god relive his day of error, understanding—the harvest of his daring—came to him: "understanding
came/ Of a fatal condemnation." The scales fell from his eyes
the same moment as in his dramatic agony, the blood scales
fell from the god's eyes, and once again restored to sanity, he
saw the error of his deed:

> Too late for joy, the Hunter stayed his hand
> The chute of truth opened from red furnaces
> And Ogun stayed his hand

> Truth, a late dawn.

Truth was a late dawn too for the men of Ire:

> Too late came a warning that a god
> Is still a god to men, and men are one
> When knowledge comes, of death.

Truth for men alas is too often a late dawn.

The secrets of "Idanre," yielded to the poet three years and
some two hundred miles later than the actual walk up Idanre,
are revealed in words addressed to the god which the poet
overhears. Ogun had grieved over the splitting of the unified
godhead. Here what he hears is a celebration of Atunda's act—
a celebration of diversity which is the essence of life and growth
rather than uniformity which is death. What Ogun heard were

> not voices whom the hour
> Of death had made all one, nor futile flight
> But the assertive act of Atunda, and he was shamed
> In recognition of the grim particular
> It will be time enough, and space, when we are dead
> To be a spoonful of the protoplasmic broth
> Cold in wind-tunnels, lava flow of nether worlds
> Deaf to thunder blind to light, comatose
> In one omni-sentient cauldron

> Time enough to abdicate to astral tidiness
> The all in one, superior annihilation of the poet's
> Diversity—

The poet too hears this justification of individuality and the diversity that it brings. It would be an act of renunciation to abandon the individuality which allows the poet to make his lonely pilgrimage. The poem, in fact, becomes a celebration of the individual will wherever it has appeared and has produced the remarkable individual whose life and thinking have changed the lives of men. Atunda, then, is no treacherous slave, but a saint in the exalted company of all divine assertions of individual will:

> All hail Saint Atunda, First revolutionary
> Grand iconoclast at genesis—and the rest in logic
> Zeus, Osiris, Jahweh, Christ in trifoliate
> Pact with creation, and the wisdom of Orunmila, Ifa
> Divining eyes, multiform

This is not a climactic assertion within the poem "Idanre" alone, but an assertion of the individual will to which much of Soyinka's work points. The dreamer—the lonely visionary—is the potential savior of his society. Only through him can society be renewed. Only through him can man take one of his forward steps.

After this climactic purgation of his grief, Ogun can depart, and the poet can return to earth. He returns to the symbolic wine-girl. She is still there keeping her lone vigil, and like all of her human kind, looking forward to the harvest—not the perverted harvest of Ogun's day of error—but a fruitful natural harvest which came:

> And Harvest came, responsive
>
> The first fruits rose from subterranean hoards
> First in our vision, corn sheaves rose over hill
> Long before the bearers, domes of eggs and flesh
> Of palm fruit, red, oil black, froth flew in sun bubbles
> Burst over throngs of golden gourds.

This is the harvest for which men pray, but of which all too often by their own contributory actions they are deprived. Such is the latent contradiction in man's nature, a contradiction he shares with Ogun. "Idanre" is a major poetic expression of some of the pervading themes in Soyinka's work.

IX   Poems From Prison

Wole Soyinka was detained in prison from August, 1967, until
1970. In 1969 Rex Collings published two poems written in
prison. There was no doubt in the minds of those who were
familiar with Soyinka's work that the poems were his. The characteristic of making the immediate environment yield larger
meanings, the ability to light upon the apt fixing image, the
economical style were all there. But more importantly, and to
the great relief of his admirers, the ideas were also there:
the assertion of the individual will; the lonely figure separate,
yet a part of the society, even a victim of the society; the concern
for that society even as one groans under it. All these appear in
the *Poems From Prison.*

Totally different in effect though it is, the technique of "Live
Burial" reminds of that of "Telephone Conversation"—the banter-
ing surface tone lightly spread over the graver implications
beneath. Here, however, the surface is more often broken by
the sinister undertones. The graver and more sinister suggestions
start from the stark first stanza where the narrow confinement
"Sixteen paces/ By twenty-three" constitutes a lingering assault—
"siege"—against the prisoner's "sanity." The economy of the
statement of that first stanza is as good as anything Soyinka
produced outside prison. Its starkness is symbolically reflective
of the prisoner's deprived state.

The second stanza is based on the Antigone story. The prisoner
becomes Haemon who has allied himself with his lover Antigone
against his own father Creon. The analogy has aptness. The
son allying himself with an outsider becomes even more hated
than the outsider. His attempt to "unearth/ Corpses of Yester
Year" is doubly embarrassing because he is a member of the
family. The sentence in stanza 3—"Seal him Live/ In the same
necropolis"—is not a literal echo of Antigone where Haemon's
entry into Antigone's cave and his later death were voluntary;
here the decree is from above. The prisoner is condemned to
the same fate as those whose cause he seems to espouse:

> May his ghost mistress
> Point the classic
> Route to Outsiders' Stygian mysteries.

The prisoner is not killed in our poem, only entombed—
"Sixteen paces/ By twenty-three"—and he is watched by guards

who are portrayed with a strong hint of sadism. They "thrill" at the "constipated groan" of the underexercised prisoner whose physical state is thus economically suggested. His suffering is in sharp contrast to the implied sniggers of the "voyeurs" outside as they listen to the "Muse" singing in a common key, and gloating at their sudden discovery of at least one plane of equality with him. Then comes the almost throwaway tone of the last stanza, lightly covering the chilling physical undertones of the last line: "Our plastic surgeons tend his public image." The line simultaneously suggests good public relations men piecing together clichés to keep the public happy and, more gravely, the damaged physical state of the prisoner being patched up for a public showing.

The poem has far more significance than the plight of any one prisoner. It portrays the plight of the individual who runs up against juggernaut authority—a theme which occurs all over Soyinka's work—but particularly in "The Dreamer," *The Strong Breed, Kongi's Harvest,* and *The Interpreters.* As an author Soyinka has always faced the consequence of such a stance: Eman is sacrificed by the people he tried to save (*The Strong Breed*); Sekoni is driven into insanity; the dreamer is crucified. This poem holds no more optimism for this type of figure in society. It is ironical that Soyinka has suffered in some measure the fate of so many of his "dreamers." It is cruel testimony to the integrity of his poetic vision.

At the start of the second poem, "Flowers For My Land," the poet takes up an antiwar protest song from a distant land. They ask where their flowers have gone, but their distant cry has echoes in the "here" of the poet's own land where, instead of flowers, death is being sown, so that the garlands which result are heavy "Garlands of Scavengers." The weight is the weight of guilt—the guilt which arises from man's own act of sowing death for flowers. The application to Nigeria is so obvious that it may blind us to the universality of the kind of guilt which the poem treats. The echo of the protest song is, of course, a pointer to the world outside Nigeria and a consequent broadening of the range of application.

The analogy between flowers and death is meant to juxtapose the potential for life and beauty, and the opposites for which this is exchanged. This is very starkly brought out in two successive stanzas:

Seeking
Voices of rain in sunshine
Blue kites on ivory-cloud
Towers
Smell of passing hands on mountain flowers.

These images of life, beauty, and grace soon became transformed into their opposites (while Soyinka wittily repeats the
key words) in:

I saw
Four steel kites, riders
On shrouded towers
Do you think
Their arms are spread to scatter mountain flowers?

The kites have grimly become planes, the clouds cover, and the
mountain flowers, bombs.

In this situation—of war—voices of dissent (even when they
may also be voices of truth) are not tolerated, and this is no
specially "Nigerian" situation. The tares are all too commonly
in a position to withhold possession of the lawns from the flowers.
In the exigencies of the present, reason and long-term interests
are suppressed and crushed. It is against the senselessness of
such a situation that the poem makes its ironic call for unity
of the weak—"the mangled kind." Even the words of the call
carry in themselves an anticipatory frustration. The tone of the
parody "Orphans of the world/ ignite" is ironic.

These two poems represent a triumph of the universal mind
over the limitations and the frustrations of a purely local situation, even prison. Even in prison Soyinka's mind can still reach
back into time and outward to the rest of the world to view the
plight of man, the victim of his own stupidity.

Soyinka's poetry must not be interpreted in too limited a sense.
He may be starting from fairly obviously indentifiable points—
his own imprisonment and the Nigerian war in these two poems—
but his concern is with the values he has always been preoccupied
with: truth as it is painfully discovered by the individual; the
struggle to remain faithful to this truth; the need for self-
sacrifice to enhance the truth; the consciousness that even when
the mind is resolute, the body sometimes falters when the ultimate price is demanded.

X "*Requiem*"

"Requiem" first appeared in the first edition of Moore and Beier's *Modern Poetry From Africa* (1963), but was not included in their revised edition of 1968. Soyinka himself leaves it out of the *Idanre* collection even though its somber mood seems to fit that collection's prevailing mood of gray. It exhibits a number of Soyinka touches. It opens with a fittingly delicate representation of barely perceptible intimations of life after death and of a continuing relationship with the dead, through a deft selection of images:

> You leave your faint depressions
> Skim-flying still, on the still pond's surface
> Where darkness crouches, egret wings
> Your love is as gossamer. . . .

The barely perceptible and evanescent ripple left by the merest touch of the flying bird, leaving the pond unruffled enough for the epithet "still" to continue to apply, is the best image I have seen used to express continuing contact between the living and the dead—a belief founded more on hope than on experience, yet strong and persistent for all that.

The whole subject itself—the probing of the twilight area between life and death—is familiar in the poet's other work. He touches on this in "Abiku," "The Hunchback of Dugbe," and "A First Deathday" where he uses the belief of the continuity of life without actually trying to portray contact across the barrier. For *The Road*, Soyinka provides a human bridge in the *Agemo* phase which "includes the passage of transition to the divine essence" (note "For the Producer," *The Road*). But since the link—Murano—is dumb, there is not much enlightened communication with the other world. It is this difficult task of portraying credibly this communion with the dead which "Requiem" attempts.

The results are not to me satisfactory, mainly because many of the images suggest distracting rather than informing ideas, a situation not often encountered in the work of a poet whose main strength lies in his extraordinary gift for choosing and organizing the significantly suggestive images. (Even here in sections—as the opening section shows—this extraordinary gift appears.) In the fourth section, which employs Soyinka's familiar technique of changing the form of the verb, there is an uncertainty—in my mind at least—as to when in the context of the whole poem the events in the section take place. Did the opening invitation end because "Storm whispers swayed you outward," etc.? Do "watched" and "swayed" refer to the same dramatic time? Uncertainties such as these impaired my reading of the poem.

Viewed from the point of view of bulk—by itself a doubtful criterion—Soyinka's corpus of poems is not very large. (In terms of the output of African poets, it is still larger than most.) From the point of view of sustained quality, the potency of his ideas and both the depth and urgency of its message it is probably the most important corpus up to now. Poetry has not yet saved the world, and it is unlikely that even if Soyinka's poetry were to be widely read, it would save Africa. It still needs—along with the rest of his work—to be read very widely by those in power as well as by those who put them in power, but especially by the young. For Soyinka's work has all the civilizing influence of a combination of vibrant ideas with art.

CHAPTER 4

The Interpreters

Although *The Interpreters* is a first novel, it comes in Soyinka's work after a number of remarkable plays and a corpus of distinguished poems which had cleared the hurdles of a literary apprenticeship. The year of the novel's publication, 1965, also saw the first production of *The Road* at the Commonwealth Arts Festival in London, and of two radio plays, *Camwood on the Leaves* (March), and *The Detainee* (September) on the BBC. By that year, *The Strong Breed, The Swamp Dwellers, Brother Jero, The Lion and the Jewel,* and *A Dance of the Forests* had all appeared. The published poetry ranged from the light satirical "Telephone Conversation" to the somber probings of life after death in "Requiem." The author of this first novel was thus no new writer, and the work shows by its complexity and literary accomplishment the results of a preceding period of intense literary activity.

In a review in *The New African,* Gerald Moore calls the novel "the first African novel that has a texture of real complexity and depth." This judgment certainly isolates two of the principal characteristics of the work. The complexity is evident in the actual language—syntax, imagery, and so on—as well as in the dense interlocking of psyches, motives, and incidents. Depth is produced by a technique of probing through external manifestations back into preceding histories and backgrounds, to other times and other places. The technique of broken chronology particularly enhances this deepening and widening of the scope of the novel as the author dives below the tip of the iceberg and goes under and around it. For time clues (of which there are some) he generally substitutes thematic links between sections of the novel to produce seemingly sudden chronological jumps which are, however, seldom capricious but rather, essential and illuminating.

The chronological time covered by sizable sections of the novel is sometimes on close examination quite brief. As Mrs.

Anne-Marie Heywood observes in some unpublished notes on
the novel, "The first seven chapters are memories and reflections
laced into the events of less than twenty-four hours." This is
the amount of time which elapses between the nightclub scene
and the two contrasted funerals of Sir Derinola and the elder
of Lazarus' Church. This span covers a hundred and thirteen
pages of the story within which the backgrounds and relationships of the friends—"the new generation of interpreters"—have
emerged through flashbacks thematically tied to the contemporary narration. These flashbacks cover whole life spans of some
of the characters.

Almost as soon as the novel opens it dives back into time.
In the wet, dripping atmosphere of the Lagos nightclub, Egbo
sits staring at a "talkative puddle," and his mind goes back to
a significant journey by water. The thematic link here is water,
the puddle in the nightclub receding into "the still water of the
creek" which was the scene of the crucial journey. Through this
transition Egbo's significant "choice" is portrayed. Instead of
opting for the traditional pattern of life by which he could
succeed (even displace) his maternal grandfather on the throne
of Osa—the progressives of the kingdom were all for this—he
had opted to go "with the tide" and continue his routine and
comfortable job at the Foreign Office.

Egbo's choice is in one sense a personal one—"the warlord
of the creeks against the dull grey filing cabinet faces of the
foreign office" (p. 12). In another sense it is a more fundamental
choice involving a lot more than his personal fortunes, and in
this sense it mirrors the changing society in which the novel is
set, and the necessity for choice which it presents. Egbo's choice
involves a break with the traditional. He is conscious of this;
not only of the luxury of polygamy—"I've thought of that. Long
and seriously" (p. 14)—but also of the opportunities which his
royal position coupled with his enlightenment would offer him—
"By example to convert the world." The traditional life has its
excitements and rewards, but also its responsibilities; and he
is by no means certain that he has the equipment to start from
the traditional base and still convert the world. In a later return
to the choice, his uncertainties about his fitness for the role of
traditional ruler are more clearly revealed. His present job is
safe; he can evaluate its demands and can be reassured by its
routine nature. It requires, as he sees it, "less of resources into

which a man must needs drill, risky like oil-well; it could be
dry and he would find it out at the moment when his presumption
most needed it" (p. 119). Egbo's choice, over which he "broods"
continually because he more than suspects it is cowardly, is to
"go with the tide," a phrase which conveniently carries its own
criticism.

Egbo's choice involves a struggle; it involves facing issues
and taking decisions. Essentially he is on his own, and in this
he represents his generation who are all facing a new world
with all the weight (but with little of the benefits) of their
traditional past. All the young interpreters are individuals trying
to make sense of their world. They are hammering out values
and codes of conduct in a world which seems to have none ready
made. Time and time again the novel portrays the essential
isolation of the new generation. Dehinwa the young career girl
is alone in the big city, away from the almost oppressive care
("blood cruelty" she calls it) and concern of her family. She has
to steer a path through all the opportunities as well as the
temptations of the big city without the support of her family.
The young unnamed university girl has to bear the consequences
of her pregnancy alone. Her message to the father of her expected
child—significantly another of her own generation—conveys the
loneliness of her position, and the enormous burden of such
loneliness. In the words of Bandele, the message to Egbo is
simple, shorn of all dramatics, but firm: "when you are sure
what you want to do you are to tell me and I will pass it on.
And I am supposed to tell you that you are under no obligation"
(p. 242). The girl has made what in the social context of the
novel is a staggering decision to take full responsibility for her
pregnancy and continue to battle with life alone if necessary.
She will return to the university.

Similar choices face all the "interpreters" and it is this necessity
to make choices, to carve paths—even wrong or uncomfortable
ones—which distinguishes them from other members of the
society who float along without any real values, or whose choices
have been made for them. No doubt Egbo's agony is born of
the recognition that he too seems merely to be going with the
tide. But, just to conclude these remarks on Egbo, he has further
choices. He has to make a decision to accept his responsibilities
and desert Simi—whose physical charms are still undiminished.
He has to give something up since it is clearly impossible for

him to go on satisfying his body with Simi and his mind with
"this . . . the new woman of my generation" (p. 235). He is
shown on the brink of a decision with the scales delicately tipped
in favor of the new woman who ironically is absent at the crucial
time. Egbo's plight is representative of that of all the interpreters.

There is stress and tension in the lives of the friends who make
up the group of interpreters, but in none is this more clearly
shown than in Sekoni's life which after all is the only one which
is complete in that he dies in the course of the novel. The portrayal of Sekoni is extraordinarily compact and powerful. One
intense passage covering about five pages (pp. 26-31) sweeps
him dramatically from the deck of the ship bringing him home
bursting with dreams to a mental hospital, while his dreams
(symbolized by his ingenious power station) lie in ruins, battered by his own frustrated hands. Sekoni's inner intensity—he
is the most religious of the interpreters—is effectively conveyed
by the stutter which his creator gives him. There always seems
to be more inside him than the stutter permits to come out. He
is better when he is not speaking, and Soyinka's prose rises to
a peak of intensity as he portrays Sekoni's dreams:

Sekoni, qualified engineer, had looked over the railings every day
of his sea voyage home. And the sea sprays built him bridges and
hospitals, and the large trailing furrow became a deafening waterfall
defying human will until he gathered it between his fingers, made
the water run in the lower channels of his palm, directing it against
the primeval giants on the forest banks. And he closed his palms
again, cradling the surge of power. Once he sat on a tall water
spout high above the tallest trees and beyond low clouds. Across
his sight in endless mammoth rolls, columns of rock, petrifactions of
divine droppings from eternity. If the mountain won't come, if the
mountain won't come, then let us to the mountains now, in the
name of Mohammed! So he opened his palm to the gurgle of power
from the charging prisoner, shafts of power nudged the monolith
along the fissures, little gasps of organic ecstasy and paths were
opened, and the brooding matriarchs surrendered all their strength,
lay in neat geometric patterns at his feet. . . . (p. 26)

The language here combines reality with fantasy. The energy
of the prose suitably conveys the dimensions of the work to be
accomplished. It also dramatizes the matching imagination of
Sekoni for the task. The effect is one of a creation myth with
Sekoni in the position of the all-powerful creator. Both the vast

potential of the land and the vast strength needed to harness it are present. The contrast between this size and strength on the one hand and the puniness and triviality of the tasks Sekoni is assigned when he actually takes up his post—"applications for leave," "bicycle advance" and so on—is a quick recipe for disaster. Five pages or so later, Sekoni is, and convincingly so, in a mental hospital. A mental breakdown is almost inevitable in the circumstances. Because Sekoni is the most intense, his frustrations are of greater dimensions. He really goes through the furnace.

It is significant that when he turns to art, his masterpiece (a piece of sculpture) is a sinewy manifestation of inner strength and intensity: "Taut sinews, nearly agonising in excess tension, a bunched python caught at the instant of easing out, the balance of strangulation before release, it was all electricity and strain" (p. 99). It is produced in a frenzy of activity, "as if time stood in his way" (p. 100)—as indeed it did, for he died soon after. Both Sekoni and his "wrestler" in their way are symbolic of the struggle in which the generation is involved (if it cares to be involved). The inspiration for the statue had indeed been conflict—a nightclub brawl. Sekoni had created an abiding masterpiece out of a fairly trivial piece of mundane experience. In a similar way, the total meaning of life for Soyinka's young men is to be painfully pieced together out of the trivia and the routines of existence—sexual encounters, riotous nights at the night club, cocktail parties, interviews for jobs, encounters with corrupt politicians, witnessing the chasing of thieves, attempts at formal philosophical formulations, attempts at artistic expression, teaching university classes and marking uninspired essays, witnessing gory road accidents, being bereft of friends by death, looking for the residual presences of the ancient gods in their midst, trying to make sense of the claims of new religious manifestations. Through all these, men are to make a coherence of the jumble that is life. Egbo in particular, because he has this special feeling that he has opted for a purposeless life, feels the need for the contemplation of life's experiences. This is why his nature shrine is so valuable to him:

I come here often to draw upon that gift and be reprieved. I find I need it more than all my friends, they are all busy doing something, but I seem to go from one event to the other. As if life was nothing but experience. . . . (p. 133)

Whether through art or through meaningful relationships, each of the young people is to work out some sort of resolution—even in death—of their experiences.

Kola looks to art for his fulfilment and comes to the painful realization that, unlike Sekoni, he is no artist; this in itself is a valuable if painful piece of self-knowledge: "I am not really an artist. I never set out to be one. But I understand the nature of art and so I make an excellent teacher of art" (p. 27). Beside the wrestler, his Pantheon is mere "weight." His face-saving "I never set out to be" is rather belied by his jealousy (which he honestly admits) at the obvious superiority of Sekoni's work (p. 100). His realization of his limitations in spite of his hard work is yet another manifestation of the basic honesty of the interpreters. His admission of his feelings for Monica brings with it a new decision, a choice which holds some promise of the fulfilment which he has failed to find in art.

Sagoe eventually finds a similar anchor in Dehinwa whom he will marry. In return for Dehinwa's surrender, he has promised to burn his "Books of Enlightenment." Sagoe had elevated his rather superficial thoughts on "Voidancy" into a philosophy from which he sought escape from the trials of existence. His resort to these "Books" on one difficult occasion is instructive. Soyinka uses their different reactions to the death of Sekoni as a significant index to the character of each of the young men. Sagoe had drenched himself in beer and vomit for a week and had then sought refuge in a random page from this book. It is clear that this is mere escapism, and this Sagoe implicitly acknowledges when he trades his book and its philosophy for a settled relationship with Dehinwa.

Bandele functions among his friends as a prod for their consciences. It is significant that it was in response to his question "which way?" that Egbo made his choice: "with the tide" (p. 13). He is generally reticent but springs into action when this is necessary. In the opening nightclub scene he had used his prehensile limbs most effectively to rescue chairs and tables from the rain (p. 7), and in a later brawl, it was he who had almost miraculously felled and trussed up the threatening thug (p. 219). He is the consoler; this is his role, significantly, at the death of Sekoni. Egbo escaped to his shrine, Sagoe into drink, but "To Bandele fell the agony of consoling Alhaji Sekoni" (p. 156). This is typical. He tries to reconcile Egbo with his choice

(p. 120) and is always something of a reconciler. His ability to tolerate the company of people he really finds unbearable surprises even his friends (p. 203). Even to the objectionable Faseyi he is "guardian uncle" (p. 206) and "god-father." However, his probings and even his silences sometimes make his friends bristle or feel uneasy. (This is the role of a conscience.) He certainly affects Kola in this way when the latter is struggling not only with his Pantheon but with his feelings for Monica, and a possible decision to step in and take her away from her husband Ayo Faseyi. Bandele's entry throws him on the defensive: "The door opened again and Bandele entered," throwing Kola instantly on his guard, almost belligerent, "If you have come to start..." (p. 218).

As the various relationships move uncomfortably to some sort of resolution toward the end of the book, the tall, towering figure of Bandele becomes increasingly detached from his companions and seems to assume the role of a divine judge. Some of Soyinka's descriptions of him at the end clearly suggest this: "Bandele came in again, a palace housepost carved of ironwood." The detached aloofness of a carving reflects his new role of touchstone and objective point of reference. Carving supplies other significant pictures of him, symbolizing some sort of ultimate reality against which acts and decision have to be measured: "It was as if he had neither pity nor indulgence, and yet the opposite was true.... And Bandele held himself unyielding, like the staff of Ogboni, rigid in a single casting.... Bandele sat like a timeless image brooding over lesser beings" (p. 244). It is through the eyes of this timeless arbiter which Bandele seems to have become, that events like the death of Noah (which Golder seems to be getting away with), the desertion of Simi by Egbo for "the new woman of my generation" (p. 255), the eventual equities of this girl's own case, have to be eventually viewed. It is he who with the full authority of his new position proclaims the final curse on the sneering, uncompassionate old guard—old and young: "Bandele, old and immutable as the royal mothers of Benin throne, old and cruel as the *Ogboni* in conclave pronouncing the Word. 'I hope you all live to bury your daughters'" (p. 251).

The group which Bandele so solemnly curses represents (with other characters) the establishment against which the young interpreters continually bruise themselves in their individualistic adventures in the society. Ayo Faseyi who is almost pathologically anxious to establish himself as a member of this power group gives a reasonable sample of its membership as he complains of the damage his wife has done to his candidature: "Do you know a Minister was present. Yes, and one or two other VIPs. Oguazor knows people, you know. I saw four corporation chairmen there, and some permanent Secretaries" (p. 202). Faseyi here characteristically lists people by their titles. In this society, this is all that matters—the front that is presented to the world. So long as this front is starched and ironed, it does not seem to matter what lies behind. It is this lack of concern for essentials, this substitution of an appearance of honor and morality for the thing itself, that the novel continually satirizes.

Professor Oguazor, the novel's main satirical butt of the Ibadan establishment, is symbolically placed in a house decorated with plastic fruit and flowers, in which these objects take the place of real ones. The house is, in a phrase which aptly represents the novel's attitude, "The Petrified Forest." Sagoe enthusiastically approaches the inviting basket of fruit—"there is no fruit in the world to beat the European apple"—only to discover its phoniness. (This is a variation of a favorite Soyinka image for the negation of the forces of life—the aborted harvest.[1]) The falsity of the façade is imaged as an unnatural substitution of death for life: "A glaze for the warmth of life and succulence" (p. 140). This unnaturalness, suggested by the image of the plastic fruit, is exemplified by Professor Oguazor's act of unnaturally hiding away his illegitimate daughter—"the plastic apple of his eye"—in a private school in Islington. ("Plastic" once again devalues any natural feelings that Oguazor as father might have had for the child.) Having neatly tucked his natural child away, Oguazor can now present to the respectable world a nicely laundered façade of virtue. He can take the most uncompromising line of "meral" rectitude against the young university girl and her partner if he can be found: "Well, see that he is expelled of course. He deserves nothing less. . . . The college cannot afford to herve its name dragged down by the meral terpitude of irresponsible young men. The younger generation is too merally corrupt" (p. 250). Oguazor's real unfitness to make judgments of this kind, contrasted with his power to do so because of his position in the society, is at the heart of the satire in the novel.

This is also the basis of the satire implied in the treatment of Sir Derinola, the judge. On the bench he is a pillar of rectitude, but he is not above taking petty bribes, hiding behind the more obviously corrupt front of the crooked politician Chief Winsala. The demolition of the façade is accomplished in the novel by both fantasy and fact. In fantasy, Sir Derinola appears in Sagoe's hangover daydream, symbolically naked, stripped of all his respectable façade of robes and wig, but, to make the picture truly comic, dressed in a pair of Dehinwa's brassieres—"For the medals young man. The medals. They pin something on you when they give you a knighthood you know." The incongruity of the medals against the nakedness of Sir Derinola is a physical image of his unfitness for the honor that the medals imply. In another episode, the exposure in fantasy is dramatized in fact when Sir Derinola is confronted by Sagoe in circumstances which establish conclusively his involvement in Chief Winsala's attempt to extract a bribe. The public image suffers a crushing blow, "But above all, Sir Derinola was truly paralysed at the confrontation of a future image, and could not move to help. Now he saw Sagoe move forward, and tried to shrink back behind the palm. They gazed into each other, all subterfuge pointless. It was Sagoe who took his eyes away" (p. 92).

The satire, particularized here through Sir Derinola, is more general. It is the whole society—indeed the novel suggests the whole "civilised" world—which is characterized by this hypocrisy and moral confusion. The chase of the young thief Noah, in chapter 8, becomes a farce in which the crowd—which in the name of virtue bears down on the young thief—is itself made up of thieves: "So the crowd bore through him, swarmed into the car park, slipped on wet tar and rose muddy and gay, snatched a handbag or two from sheer opportunity and blacked the grounds before the squat lumpy factory that was Hotel Excelsior" (p. 114). The whole business of justice has become a game in which the sword is in the hands of thieves. As the passage goes on, the whole society becomes involved in the satire on this particular crowd: "Run, you little thief or the bigger thieves will pass a law against your existence as a menace to society . . . run, Barabbas from the same crowd which will reform tomorrow and cheer the larger thief returning from his twentieth Economic Mission and pluck his train from the mud, dog-wise, in their teeth" (p. 114). The values of the whole society have

become inverted; morality has become redefined, a point which
is bitingly made when the chase of the thief is ironically called
"a moral demonstration" (p. 114).

The inhumanity displayed by Oguazor and his company toward
the young pregnant girl is paralleled by the chase of the thief.
It is this same essential inhumanity that characterizes the treatment of Sekoni. He is brought to mental collapse while the
cynical Chairman of the Electricity Board actually makes money
out of his condemned power station. The sheer comedy of some
of the episodes through which society is satirized—the Oguazor
party, for example—should not obscure the basic inhumanity
which the attitude involves. To protect the phony façade, those
who do not conform are crushed—"expelled," sentenced, driven
to insanity. The satire is indeed serious, and *The Interpreters*
is a most serious novel in spite of its cloak of comedy. This is
a characteristic which it shares with Soyinka's comic plays.

The primary society with which the novel is concerned is contemporary Nigeria in which, although the ancient traditional
life still makes its appearance, the predominant impression is of
a society in the grips of a turbulent modernity. Its institutions—
universities, hotels, churches, nightclubs, newspapers, and so
on—show an uneasy blend of influences. Somewhere in the background linger the numinous presences of the old gods, manifesting
themselves intangibly but still effectively by the banks of the
Oshun and Ogun, and, as though the new generation is straining
back to something to hold on to, in the Pantheon of Kola's canvas.
The *apala* band asserts itself in the Lagos nightclub when the
western saxophones and trumpets have succumbed to the rain,
but the nightclub itself—the Cambana—is a curiously uncertain
place. It is a pale imitation of an American evocation of Africa—
"in the States they really go to town" (p. 157). The paints of the
fire-eater are done in "designs which he had perhaps copied from
the film of Tarzan's adventures with the Authentic Cobra Maidens
of Kokokabura" (p. 158). Lazarus' church, while showing perhaps a little more independence with its defiantly African
rhythms, manifests its uncertainties in the substandard English
of the Elder: "Brother Ezra was our oldest man. On his wise head
we rely on for so many advices, so many of our problem that
we have to deal with" (p. 170). When Chief Winsala is caught
without the price of the schnapps he has been guzzling in the
Hotel Excelsior, it is in the words of traditional wisdom that he

mirrors his position to himself and implicitly reproves himself for thus exposing himself: "*Agba n't'ara* . . . it is no matter for rejoicing when a child sees his father naked, *l'ogolonto*. Agba n't'ara. The wise eunuch keeps from women; the hungry clerk dons coat over his narrow belt and who will say his belly is flat? But when *elegungun* is unmasked in the market, can he then ask *egbe* to snatch him into the safety of *igbale?* Won't they tell him the grove is meant only for keepers of mystery?" (p. 92). The point here is that Winsala has been caught in a modern situation—a company director fishing for a bribe—but in the moment of stress he recalls the ancient rules of conduct which he has violated in the process. It is interesting that the Chief seems to regret only his temporary disgrace, not the basic reason for it, namely, his dishonesty. This curious intrusion of the old Africa into the new is interesting.

Sometimes there is little mutual comprehension between the old and the new. Dehinwa's mother and aunt are in a totally incomprehensible world when they visit her in her flat in the city, and she turns up with a drunken man who proceeds to go to sleep on her bed. Dehinwa too, having absorbed the detached attitudes of the city, has forgotten that in traditional life everybody's business is everybody's business as this exchange shows:

"But mamma, you shouldn't listen to that kind of talk. Next time tell them to mind their business." The aunt left her mouth open in mid-swallow. "What did the child say? Tell people to mind their own business when it is their love for your mother that prompts them to speak?" (p. 37)

In such ways do the old and the new Africa in this fluid society sometimes confront, sometimes uneasily blend with each other in the novel.

In the lives of individuals even in the new Africa, the old Africa could never be totally ignored. Even the young interpreters find that they have to take old Africa into account in the formulation of their new values. The old refuses to be bodily jettisoned. Sagoe fondly hoped that he could shed his family and carve out a life for himself as an individual in the city. His plan on his return from his studies abroad was to settle himself first, then "a brief courtesy visit and then finish. Every man to his own business." Bandele, the wise one, had promptly indicated that this was not as easy as it sounded: "Bandele shook his head, 'That is not easy'" (p. 90). (That courtesy visit would have undone him anyway.) Egbo's attempts to wrench himself free of the past is no more successful. The past, history, tradition, and the dead will never let him go, even when he has seemingly decided against committing himself to his traditional role as king of Osa. The tyranny of the past hangs over him, and he is irritated by it: "It [the past] should be dead. And I don't just mean bodily extinction. No, what I refer to is the existing fossil within society, the dead branches on a living tree, the dead runs on the bole. When people die, in one sense or in the other, it should not matter what they were to us. They owe the living a duty to be forgotten quickly, usefully. Believe me, the dead should have no faces" (p. 120). The fact is, as the novel reminds us, they have.

Egbo's irritation reflects the uneasy quality of a society which has not completely come to terms with itself. It is in this uncertain atmosphere that corruption, tribalism, window-dressing hypocrisy, and moral uncertainty flourish. It is through all these uncertainties that the interpreters seek a path; it is in formal recognition of the fact that the past cannot be disregarded in this search that they slaughter a black goat at the dedication of Sekoni's work.

The primary society treated is Nigeria, but the society is shown in bustling contact with the wider world. Not only do managing directors circle the world on economic missions, but Germans, Americans, Englishmen flow in and out of the society and widen the area of experience which the novel covers. The interpreters themselves have studied abroad. Artifacts from the outside world are introduced, sometimes satirically, throughout the novel. The Managing Director's "pachydermous radiogram" (p. 78) is not only an index of his own faulty taste and misplaced values—"only the radio was ever used, and that just for the news" (p. 75)— but the circumstances of its purchase in Germany when the Director tries to lure the sales girl to his hotel underlines the satire. The executive toilet ornately furnished with fittings from Switzerland but housed in a decayed building in the middle of a slum, the large American cars, are all used to point to a certain vulgar ostentation against which Sagoe protests by perversely riding only a bicycle.

Not only the artifacts, but people from other places widen

the novel's canvas. Joe Golder, Pinkshore, Peter the German-American, even Monica (who, however, becomes a part of the Nigerian scene) function in this way. Pinkshore is an Englishman who has accepted the fact of political independence and realizes that things have changed and that black men now have to be humored by white men: "it was a good thing to perform small services for this new black élite which he secretly despised but damn it all if the asses are susceptible to fawning and flattery let's give it them and get what we can out of them while the going is good" (p. 149). The satire is double-edged, cutting both the black élite and the insincere foreigners.

Joe Golder is even more fruitfully used as a vehicle of double-edged satire. He becomes a representative of the American dilemma. He himself is of a complexion that would pass for white, but having Negro blood in him, he is, in American terms, black. Golder overcompensates by being passionately and aggressively black. He tortures himself in the sun trying to darken his stubborn complexion, and he urges Kola to represent him in the Pantheon in the blackest black: "For God's sake, blacken me. Make me the blackest black blackness in your pantheon" (p. 217). Golder's predicament is compounded by the fact that he is also a homosexual. This conflict of races and of sexes in the one man produces a figure who hovers between comedy and tragedy. His hideous attempts to blacken himself may be comic, but it is comedy born out of the victim's real pain. There is real tragedy also. The racial conflict within him had turned him against his father whom he drove to suicide. His sexual aberration leads directly to the death of Noah. From this background of tragedy Golder's voice rises in the apt Negro spiritual whose lines—with which Soyinka punctuates his presentation of other matters—symbolize not only Golder's own personal isolation but also the essential loneliness of each of the seekers: "Sometimes I feel like a motherless child. . . ."

A list of topics which the novel covers either substantially or glancingly would almost match the number of its pages. Through glancing allusions, the canvas stretches from America to Chiang Kai-shek's "American China." In the realm of human relations, racialism, tribalism (Dehinwa's mother is scandalized at the idea of her daughter going out with a Gambari), religious intolerance (Sekoni and his father), homosexuality, different kinds of sexual relations, various kinds of monogamy, and polygamy, love—are all explored. The satire encompasses corruption, political thuggery, bribery, universities (undergraduates as well as their teachers), religion, war, and a host of other topics. All this Soyinka harmonizes into a novel of true artistic distinction. It mirrors in its energy the vitality of its setting, and in its restless style the agonies through which the immediate society and the world must go if it is to produce some kind of solution to its myriad problems. The novel makes few assertions, but it probes and exposes themes for judgment.

The young interpreters, as distinct from others in the novel who are self-satisfied and complacent, are engaged in a search for individual solutions without the automatic props of the old sheltered way of life or any substitute for it in the modern world. They have to cut their way through a maze consisting of their own personal resources and limitations and the opportunities offered by their immediate environment of Nigeria, but ultimately of the whole modern world, through friendship and love, through hatred, intolerance, and corruption. The novel is an artistic realization of the opportunities as well as of the awful responsibilities of being an individual on his own in a maze of a world.

Notes and References

Chapter One

1. *The Forest of a Thousand Daemons* (Nelson, 1968), p. 4.
2. *Five Plays* (Oxford, 1964), p. 50.
3. D. W. Jefferson, ed., *The Morality of Art* (London: Routledge and Kegan Paul, 1965).
4. *Yoruba Culture* (Ife and London, 1966), p. 20.
5. *The Forest of a Thousand Daemons*, p. 3.
6. Ojo, *Yoruba Culture*, p. 182.
7. *The Morality of Art*, p. 120.
8. Published by *Nigeria Magazine* (Lagos, 1957, 1959).
9. Mr. Soyinka kindly gave me a copy of the mimeographed pamphlet which records the occasion.
10. Published by *Nigeria Magazine* (Lagos, 1959).
11. "The Traditional Content of the Plays of Wole Soyinka," *African Literature Today*, no. 4 (1970), p. 8.
12. Interview, *Spear* (May, 1966), p. 19.
13. For a fuller discussion, see pp. 117-19 below.
14. See pp. 59-60 below.
15. *Spear* (May, 1966), p. 16.
16. *Ibid.*, p. 20.
17. *Five Plays*, p. 144.
18. Jefferson, *The Morality of Art*, p. 133.

Chapter Two

1. The resemblance between Lakunle and Joyce Cary's *Mr. Johnson* is striking.
2. *Long Drums and Cannons* (London: Macmillan, 1968), p. 45.
3. I differ here from Margaret Laurence who writes of the poet: "The poet lets his novice fall to his death in rescuing the queen's canary from the roof-top" (*Long Drums*, p. 37).
4. Soyinka, "The Writer in a Modern African State," *The Writer in Modern Africa*, ed. Per Wastberg (Uppsala, 1968), p. 20.
5. For a summary of the different readings of Ulli Beier, Una Maclean, and Margaret Laurence's own interpretation, see the latter's *Long Drums and Cannons*, especially page 43.
6. This perilous dance, for which Soyinka had to substitute a different tableau in the alternative ending of the play, is done by

173

professional dancers in many parts of West Africa. Geoffrey Gorer describes such a dance in *Africa Dances* (London: Faber, 1935), p. 317.

7. Broadcast in the BBC African Service, March, 1965.

8. See Margaret Laurence, *Long Drums and Cannons,* p. 63.

9. O.U.P., Three Crowns ed. (1967).

10. "The Traditional Content of the Plays of Wole Soyinka," *African Literature Today*, no. 4. This is an important article on Soyinka from which, even when I depart from its interpretations, I have benefited.

11. "Thick, coarse, woven cloth," p. 8.

12. The figure of Socrates is invoked again in *Madmen and Specialists*. See p. 105.

13. Oyin Ogunba sees the whole dirge of *ege* as "a dance of the death of tradition itself"—"The Traditional Content of the Plays of Wole Soyinka," *African Literature Today*, no. 4, p. 9.

14. Once again a biblical tableau is evoked—that of the sick woman touching the hem of Christ's garment.

15. "Flowers from my Land" in *Poems From Prison* (London: Rex Collings Ltd., 1969).

16. The head of St. John on a platter is a biblical parallel.

17. Broadcast BBC African Service, September, 1965, otherwise unpublished.

18. The play was unpublished at the time of writing. These notes were based on a mimeograph version kindly given to me by the author.

19. *Iya* is Yoruba for Mother.

Chapter Three

1. See in particular "And after the Narcissist," *African Forum* and "The Fourth Stage" in D. W. Jefferson, ed., *The Morality of Art* (Routledge and Kegan Paul, 1965).

2. This is the version in Francess Ademola's *Reflections* (A.U.P., 1962) and in the first edition of Moore and Beier, *Modern Poems from Africa* (1963).

3. For a fuller examination of the harvest image see E. Jones, "The Harvest Image in 'Idanre,'" *African Literature Today*, no. 6.

Chapter Four

1. See E. Jones, "The Harvest Image in 'Idanre,'" *op. cit.*

Selected Bibliography

PRIMARY SOURCES
(arranged chronologically)

1. Poetry:

"Two in London": "The Immigrant" and "The Other Immigrant"
African Treasury, ed. Langston Hughes. London: Gollancz, 1961.
"Telephone Conversation"
"Death in the Dawn"
"Prisoner," *Reflections*, ed. Francess Ademola. Lagos: African Universities Press, 1962.
"Telephone Conversation"
"Death in the Dawn"
"Requiem"
"Prisoner"
"I think it Rains"
"Season"
"Night"
"Abiku"
Modern Poetry From Africa. London: Penguin, 1963.
"For now the sun moves"
"Lament for the rains"
"Oriki Emu" / "Praise of Palm Wine"
"Egun" / "Maledictions"
"Alimotu adengbe" / "Alimotu of the golden gourd," *Proceedings of the First Rites of the Harmattan Solstice* (mimeograph). Lagos, 1966.
Idanre and Other Poems. London: Methuen, 1967.
Poems From Prison. London: Rex Collings Ltd., 1969.

2. Short Stories:

"Madame Etienne's Establishment," *Gryphon* (Leeds University journal, March, 1957).
"A Tale of Two Cities," *Gryphon* (Autumn, 1957).
"A Tale of Two Cities" (a different story), *New Nigerian Forum*, no. 2 (London, 1958).

3. Essays and Articles:

"Salutations to the Gut," in *Reflections*, ed. Francess Ademola. Lagos:
  African Universities Press, 1962.
"Towards a True Nigerian Theatre," *Nigeria Magazine*, no. 75 (De-
  cember, 1962), pp. 58-60.
"Nigeria's International Film Festival, 1962," *Nigeria Magazine*, no.
  79 (December, 1963).
"The Fourth Stage," *The Morality of Art*, ed. D. W. Jefferson. London:
  Routledge and Kegan Paul, 1965.
"And After the Narcissist?," *African Forum*, I, vi (1966), 53-64.
"The Writer in a Modern African State," *The Writer in Modern
  Africa*, ed. Per Wastberg. Uppsala, 1968.

4. Plays:

A Dance of the Forests. London: Oxford University Press, 1963.
The Lion and the Jewel. London: Oxford University Press, 1963.
Three Plays. Nigeria: Mbari Publications, 1963.
Five Plays. London: Oxford University Press, 1964.
The Road. London: Oxford University Press, 1965 (had appeared
  earlier in *Gambit*).
Kongi's Harvest. London: Oxford University Press, 1967.
Three Short Plays. London: Oxford University Press, 1969.
The Strong Breed. Ibadan: Orisun Acting Editions, 1970.

5. Revues:

Before the Blackout. Ibadan: Orisun Acting Editions, 1971.

6. Novels:

The Forest of a Thousand Daemons (translation of D. O. Fagunwa's
  Ogboju Ode Ninu Igbo Irunmale). London: Nelson, 1968.
The Interpreters. London: Andre Deutsch, 1965.

SECONDARY SOURCES
(arranged alphabetically)

Starred items are considered specially helpful.

1. Books:

BEIER, ULLI. Ed. *Introduction to African Literature*. London: Long-
  mans, 1967.
————. *The Story of Sacred Wood Carvings From Small Yoruba
  Town*. Nigeria Magazine, 1957, 1959.

—————. *A Year of Sacred Festivals in One Yoruba Town.* Nigeria Magazine, 1959.

CARTEY, WILFRED J. *Whispers From a Continent.* New York: Random House, 1969.

ESSLIN, MARTIN. *Brecht: A Choice of Evils.* London: Eyre and Spottiswoode, 1959.

GLEASON, JUDITH I. *This Africa.* Evanston, Illinois: Northwestern University Press, 1965.

HUGHES, LANGSTON. *An African Treasury.* New York: Crown Publishers, 1960.

IDOWU, E. BOLAJI. *Olodumare: God in Yoruba Belief.* London: Longmans, 1962.

JAHN, JAHNHEINZ. *A History of Neo-African Literature.* Tr. Oliver Coburn and Ursula Lehrburger. London: Faber and Faber, 1966.

°LAURENCE, MARGARET. *Long Drums and Cannons.* London: Macmillan, 1968.

°MOORE, GERALD. *The Chosen Tongue.* London: Longmans, 1969.

°OJO, J. AFOLABI. *Yoruba Culture.* London: University of Ife Press and London University Press, 1966.

RAMSARAN, JOHN. *New Approaches to African Literature.* Ibadan: Ibadan University Press, 1965.

TAYLOR, JOHN RUSSELL. *Anger and After: A Guide to the New British Drama.* London: Methuen, 1963.

TIBBLE, ANNE. *African-English Literature.* London: P. Owen, c. 1965.

TUCKER, MARTIN. *Africa in Modern Literature.* New York: Frederick Ungar, 1967.

2. Critical Articles

ADEDEJI, J. A. "The Place of Drama in Yoruba Religious Observance," *Odu,* III, i (July, 1966), 88-94.

—————. "Form and Function of Satire in Yoruba Drama," *Odu,* IV, i (July, 1967), 61-72.

°AKARAOGUN, ALAN. "Wole Soyinka" (interview), *Spear Magazine* (May, 1966), pp. 13-19.

BANHAM, MARTIN. "African Literature II: Nigerian Dramatists in English and the Traditional Nigerian Theatre," *Journal of Commonwealth Literature,* III (1967), 97-102.

—————. "Notes on Nigerian Theatre: 1966," *Bulletin of the Association for African Literature in English,* IV (March, 1966), 31-36.

°BEIER, ULLI. "Review of *A Dance of the Forests,*" *Black Orpheus,* no. 8, 1960.

BERRY, BOYD M. "Review of *Kongi's Harvest*," *Ibadan*, no. 27 (October, 1966), pp. 53-55.

°ESSLIN, MARTIN. "Two African Playwrights," *Black Orpheus*, no. 19 (March, 1966), pp. 33-39. Also in *Introduction to African Literature*, ed. Ulli Beier. London: Longmans, 1967.

——————. "The Theatre of the Absurd," *Essays in Modern Drama*, ed. Morris Freedman. Boston: D. C. Heath & Co., 1964.

°JONES, ELDRED D. "*The Interpreters*, Reading Notes," *African Literature Today*, no. 2 (1969), pp. 42-50.

"Our Authors and Performing Artists I," *Nigeria Magazine*, no. 88 (March, 1966), pp. 57-64. Anon.

°MACLEAN, UNA. "Wole Soyinka," *Black Orpheus*, no. 15 (August, 1964), pp. 46-51.

NKOSI, LEWIS. "Soyinka's Plays Produced by South Africans," *South Africa* (May, 1966).

°OGUNBA, OYIN. "The Traditional Content of the Plays of Wole Soyinka," *African Literature Today*, nos. 4 & 5 (1970).

°WATSON, IAN. "Soyinka's International Drama," *Transition*, no. 27 (1966).

°WEST AFRICA. "Portrait: A National Dramatist," *West Africa* (December 19, 1964).

WESTCOTT, JOAN. "The Sculpture and Myths of Eshu-Elegba, The Yoruba Trickster," *Africa*, vol. 32 (1962).

°YANKOWITZ, SUSAN. "The Plays of Wole Soyinka," *African Forum*, I (Spring, 1966), 129-33.

3. Some Reviews of Productions:

The Invention:

BRIEN, ALAN. "Where Spades Are Trumps," *The Spectator* (November 6, 1959), pp. 629-30.

TIMES, THE. "African Playwright and Poet" (November 2, 1959), p. 3. Anon.

The Swamp Dwellers:

MAHOOD, M. M., AND OGUNDIPE, PHEBEAN. "Three Views of *The Swamp Dwellers*," *Ibadan*, no. 6 (June, 1969).

MACLEAN, UNA. "Words, Words, Words," *Ibadan*, no. 6 (June, 1959).

The Republican:

DAILY EXPRESS (Lagos). "Brilliant Satire by the 1960 Masks" (November 27, 1963).

Kongi's Harvest:

DUERDIN, DENNIS. "Dakar Report. A Triumph for Wole Soyinka" (review of production of *Kongi's Harvest* at Dakar Festival), *New Society* (April 28, 1964).

The Road:

BRIEN, ALAN. Review of *The Road, Sunday Telegraph* (September 19, 1965).

GILLIATT, PENELOPE. "Nigerian Original," review of the Theatre Royal production of *The Road, Observer* (September 19, 1965).

HOBSON, HAROLD. "Nigerian Drama in Premiere" (*The Road*), *Christian Science Monitor* (September 22, 1965).

ROBERTS, PETER. *The Road* (review), *Financial Times* (September 15, 1965).

SHOOTER, ERIC. Review of *The Road, Daily Telegraph* (September 15, 1965).

The Lion and the Jewel:

Christian Science Monitor. Review of *The Lion and the Jewel* (January 6, 1967).

Cultural Events in Africa. Summaries of London reviews of *The Lion and the Jewel.* No. 25 (December, 1966).

Glasgow Herald. Review of *The Lion and the Jewel* (December 17, 1966).

Jewish Chronicle. Review of *The Lion and the Jewel* (December 16, 1966).

JONES, D. A. N. "Yorubaland" (review of Royal Court production of *The Lion and the Jewel*), *New Statesman* (December 16, 1966).

KRETZNER, HERBERT. Review of *The Lion and the Jewel, Daily Express* (December 13, 1966).

LEWIS, PETER. Review of *The Lion and the Jewel, Daily Mail* London, December 13, 1966).

People, The. Review of *The Lion and the Jewel* (December 18, 1966).

Punch. Review of *The Lion and the Jewel* (December 21, 1966).

RICHARDSON, BOYCE. Review of *The Lion and the Jewel, Morning Star* (January 7, 1967).

SEYMOUR, ANTHONY. Review of *The Lion and the Jewel, Yorkshire Post* (December 13, 1966).

SHULMAN, MARTIN. Review of *The Lion and the Jewel, Evening Standard* (December 13, 1966).

Times (London). "Our Drama Critic," review of *The Lion and the Jewel* (December 13, 1966).

Times Educational Supplement. Review of *The Lion and the Jewel* (December 23, 1966).

West Africa. "Early Soyinka" (review of Royal Court production of *The Lion and the Jewel* (December 17, 1966). Anon.

YOUNG, A. J. Review of *The Lion and the Jewel, Financial Times* (December 13, 1966).

Madmen and Specialists:

New York Times. Note on *Madmen and Specialists* (August 3, 1970).

Brother Jero:

BRYDEN, RONALD. "The Voice of Africa" (includes a review of Hampstead Theatre Club production of *Brother Jero*), *Observer* (July 3, 1966).

Index